*O Allah,* send prayers upon our master Muhammad, the opener of what was closed, and the seal of what had preceded, the helper of the truth by the Truth, and the guide to Your straight path. May Allah send prayers upon his Family according to his grandeur and magnificent rank.

-SALĀT AL-FĀTĪH

TITLE: TOWARDS A BETTER DU'A
ISBN: 978-1-952306-52-5
FIRST EDITION

AUTHOR: JALĀL AL-DĪN AL-SUYŪṬĪ
TRANSLATION: TALUT IBN SULAIMAN DAWOOD

IMAM GHAZALI PUBLISHING
WWW.IMAMGHAZALI.CO
INFO@IMAMGHAZALI.CO

# Towards a Better Du'a

AL-SUYŪṬĪ'S HADITH COMPILATION ON THE RAISING OF HANDS IN DU'A & ADVICE FROM AL-ḤIṢN AL-ḤAṢĪN

Compiled by
**Jalāl al-Dīn al-Suyūṭī**

Translated by
**Talut ibn Sulaiman Dawood**

Imam Ghazali
PUBLISHING

# Table of Contents

# Imam al-Suyūṭī
## (d. 911 AH in Cairo)
Adapted from Dr. G. F. Haddad

ʻAbd al-Raḥmān ibn Kamāl al-Dīn Abī Bakr ibn Muḥammad ibn Sābiq al-Dīn Jalāl al-Dīn al-Misrī al-Suyūṭī al-Shāfiʻī al-Ashʻarī (849–911 AH), also known as Ibn al-Suyūṭī, was a *mujtahid* Imam and reformer of the tenth Islamic century. He was a prominent Hadith master, jurist, Sufi, philologist, and historian who authored works in virtually every Islamic science.

Born to a Turkish mother and a father of Persian origin, al-Suyūṭī was raised as an orphan in Cairo. He memorized the Qur'an at the age of eight, followed by several complete works of Sacred Law, fundamentals of jurisprudence, and Arabic grammar. He then devoted his life to studying the Sacred Sciences under nearly 150 sheikhs. Among them were the foremost Shāfiʻī and Ḥanafī sheikhs at the time, such as Sheikh al-Islām Sirāj al-Dīn al-Bulqīnī, with whom he studied Shāfiʻī jurisprudence; the Hadith scholar Sheikh al-Islām Sharāf al-Dīn al-Munāwī, with whom he read Qur'anic exegesis and who commented on al-Suyūṭī's *Al-Jāmi ʻ Al-Ṣaghīr* in a book entitled *Fayḍ Al-Qadīr*; and Taqī al-Dīn al-Shamani, with whom he studied Hadith and the sciences of Arabic.

Al-Suyūṭī also studied with Jalāl al-Dīn al-Maḥallī, a specialist in the principles of the law, with whom he compiled the most widespread condensed commentary on the Qur'an of our time: *Tafsīr Al-Jalālayn*. Some Ḥanafī sheikhs he studied under include Shihāb al-Dīn al-Sharmisahi, Muḥyī al Dīn al-Kafayjī, and the Hadith Master Sayf al-Dīn Qāsim ibn Qaṭlūbaghā.

In the pursuit of knowledge, al-Suyūṭī travelled to Damascus, the Hejaz, Yemen, India, and Morocco, as well as to centers of learning in Egypt such as Maḥalla, Dumyāṭ, and Fayyūm. He spent some time as the head teacher of Hadith at the Shaykhuniyya school in Cairo, at the recommendation of Imam Kamāl al-Dīn ibn al-Humām. He then took up the same position at Baybarsiyya but was dismissed due to complaints from other sheikhs whom he had replaced. After this, he retired to scholarly seclusion and did not return to the field of teaching.

In *Tārīkh Miṣr,* Ibn Iyās reveals that when al-Suyūṭī reached forty years of age, he abandoned the company of men for the solitude of the garden of al-Miqyās by the river Nile. Here, he avoided his former colleagues as though he had never known them. It was there that he authored nearly 600 books and treatises. Wealthy Muslims and princes would visit him with offers of money and gifts, but he rejected them. He also refused the sultan many times when he requested al-Suyūṭī's presence. He once said to the sultan's envoy: 'Do not ever come back to us with a gift, for in truth Allah has put an end to all such needs for us.'

Al-Suyūṭī was blessed with great success in his years of solitude, making it difficult to name a field in which he did not make outstanding contributions. Among his most prominent works is his ten-volume Hadith collection *Jam' Al-Jawāmi'* (*The Collection of Collections*); his Qur'anic exegesis *Tafsīr Al-Jalālayn* (*Commentary of the Two Jalāls*) in which he finished the second half of an uncompleted manuscript by Jalāl al-Dīn Maḥallī in only forty days; and his classic commentary on the sciences of Hadith, *Tadrīb Al-Rāwī fī Sharḥ Taqrīb Al-Nawawī* (*The Training of the Hadith Transmitter: An Exegesis of Al-Nawawī's* The Facilitation).

A giant among his contemporaries, he produced a sustained output of scholarly writings until his death at the age of sixty-two. He was buried in Hawsh Qawsūn in Cairo. In the introduction to his book *Al-Riyāḍ Al-Anīqa* on the names of the Prophet ﷺ, he wrote: 'It is my hope that Allah accepts this book and that through this book I shall gain the intercession of the Prophet ﷺ. Perhaps it shall be that Allah makes it the seal of all my works, and grants me what I have asked Him with longing, regarding the Honorable One.'

Al-Suyūṭī's student and biographer, Shams al-Dīn al-Dāwūdi al-Mālikī, the author of *Ṭabaqāt Al-Mufassirīn Al-Kubrā*, said: 'I saw the sheikh with my own eyes writing and finishing three works in one day, which he himself authored and proofread. At the same time, he was dictating hadith and replying beautifully to whatever was brought to his attention.'

Al-Suyūṭī was taken to task for his claim that he was capable of independent scholarly exertion (*ijtihād muṭlaq*). His explanation was as follows:

'I did not mean that I was similar to one of the Four Imams, but only that I was an affiliated *mujtahid* (*mujtahid muntasib*). When I reached the level of *tarjīḥ* (distinguishing the best *fatwa* inside the school), I did not contravene the *tarjīḥ* of al-Nawawī. When I reached the level of *ijtihad muṭlaq*, I did not contravene the school of al-Shāfi'ī ... There is no one in our time on the face of the Earth, from East to West, more knowledgeable than me in Hadith and the Arabic language, save al-Khidr or the pole of saints or some other *walī*, none of whom I include in my statement. And Allah knows best.'

Al-Suyūṭī also said, 'When I went on hajj, I drank Zamzam water for several matters. Among them was that I reach the level of Sheikh Sirāj al-Dīn al-Bulqīnī in Fiqh, and the level of the hafiz Ibn Hajar in Hadith.'

Below are the titles of some of al-Suyūṭī's works in print, kept in the Arabic collection of the University of Princeton in the State of New Jersey, USA. The most recent date has been given for works with more than one edition:

1. Abwāb Al-Sa'āda fī Asbāb Al-Shahāda <1987> (The Gates of Felicity in the Causes of the Witnessing to Oneness)

2. Al-Ashbāḥ wa Al-Naẓā'ir fī Furū' Al-Shāfi'iyya (Similarities in the Branches of the Law Within the Shāfi'ī School)

3. Al-Ashbāḥ wa Al-Naẓā'ir fī Al-'Arabiyya (Similarities in Arabic)

4. Al-Aḥādīth Al-Ḥisān fī Faḍl Al-Ṭaylasān <1983> (The Beautiful Narrations Concerning the Merit of the Male Head Covering)

5. Al-Fawz Al-'Aẓīm fī Liqā' Al-Karīm <1994> (The Tremendous Victory in Meeting the All-Generous)

6. Alfiyya Al-Suyūṭī Al-Naḥwiyya <1900> (The Thousand-Line Poem of Al-Suyūṭī on Philology)

7. Alfiyya Al-Suyūṭī fī Muṣṭalaḥ Al-Ḥadīth <1988> (The Thousand-Line Poem of Al-Suyūṭī on Hadith Nomenclature)

8. 'Amal Al-Yawm wa Al-Layla <1987> (Supererogatory Devotions for Each Day and Night)

9. Al-Itqān fī 'Ulūm Al-Qur'ān <1996> (Precision and Mastery in the Sciences of the Qur'an)

10. Anīs Al-Jalīs <1874> (The Familiar Companion)

11. Al-'Araj fī Al-Faraj <1988> (A Commentary on Ibn Abī al Dunyā's The Deliverance)

12. Al-Arba'ūn Ḥadīth fī Qawā'id Al-Aḥkām Al-Shar'iyya <1986> (Forty Narrations on Basic Legal Rulings)

13. Asbāb Al-Nuzūl <1983> (Causes of Qur'anic Revelation)

14. Asbāb Wurūd Al-Ḥadīth <1988> (Causes and Circumstances of Hadith)

15. Isbāl Al-Kisā' 'alā Al-Nisā' <1984> (Women and the Donning of Cover)

16. Asrār Tartīb Al-Qur'ān <1976> (The Secret in the Ordering of the Qur'an)

17. Al-Āyat al-Kubra fī Sharḥ Qiṣṣat al-Isrā' <1985> (The Great Sign: A Commentary on the Story of the Night Journey)

18. 'Ayn Al-Iṣāba fī Istidrāk 'Ā'ishah 'alā Al-Ṣaḥāba <1988> (Exactitude Itself in 'Ā'isha's Rectification of the Companions)

19. Azhār Al-Mutanāthira fī Al-Aḥādīth Al-Mutawātira <1951> (The Most Prominent of the Reports Concerning the Narrations of Mass Transmission)

20. Al-Bāhir fī Ḥukm Al-Nabī ﷺ <1987> (The Dazzling Light of the Rulings of the Prophet ﷺ)

21. Al-Bahja Al-Marḍiyya fī Sharḥ Al-Alfiyya <1980> (The Pleasing Beauty: A Commentary on the Alfiyya)

22. Bulbul Al-Rawḍa <1981> (A Chronicle on Al-Rawda)

23. Bushrā Al-Ka'īb bi Liqā' Al-Ḥabīb <1960> (The Consolation of the Sad with the Meeting of the Beloved)

24. Al-Dībāj 'alā Ṣaḥīḥ Muslim Ibn Al-Ḥajjāj <1991> (A Commentary on Ṣaḥīḥ Muslim Ibn Al-Ḥajjāj)

25. Al-Durar Al-Muntathira fī Al-Aḥādīth Al-Mushtahara <1988> (The Scattered Pearls of Famous Narrations); also published as Al-Nawafiḥ Al-'Atira fī Al-Aḥādīth Al-Mushtahara <1992> (The Fragrant Scents of Famous Narrations)

26. Al-Durr Al-Manthūr fī Al-Tafsīr bi Al-Ma'thūr (The Scattered Pearls: A Commentary of the Qur'an Based on Transmitted Reports)

27. Al-Duruj Al-Munīfa fī Al-Abā' Al-Sharīfa <1916> (The Out-

standing Entries Concerning the Ancestors of the Prophet ﷺ)

28. Faḍḍ Al-Wi'ā' fī Aḥādīth Raf' Al-Yadayn fī Al-Du'ā' <1985> (The Emptying of the Vessel Concerning Raising the Hands When Making Supplication)

29. Al-Ghurar fī Faḍā'il 'Umar <1991> (The Blazing Highlights of 'Umar's Merits)

30. Al-Ḥabā'ik fī Akhbār Al-Malā'ik <1985> (The Celestial Orbits or the Reports Concerning the Angels)

31. Ḥaqīqa Al-Sunna wa Al-Bid'a aw Al-'Amr bi Al-Ittibā' wa Al-Nahī 'an Al-Munkar <1985> (The Reality of Sunna and Innovation or the Ordering of Obedient Following and the Prohibition of Evil)

32. Al-Ḥāwī li Al-Fatāwī fī Al-Fiqh wa 'Ulūm Al-Tafsīr wa Al-Ḥadīth wa Al-Uṣūl wa Al-Naḥw wa Al-I'rāb wa Sā'ir Al-Funūn <1933> (The Collected Legal Decisions in Jurisprudence, Qur'anic Commentary, Hadith, Principles, Language, and Other Sciences)

33. Al-Ḥujaj Al-Mubayyana fī Al-Tafḍīl Bayna Makka wa Al-Madīna <1985> (The Proofs Made Manifest Concerning the Excellence of Makkah and Madinah)

34. Ḥusn Al-Maqṣid fī 'Amal Al-Mawlid <1985> (Excellence of Purpose in Celebrating the Birth of the Prophet ﷺ)

35. Ḥusn Al-Ṣamt fī Al-Ṣamt <1985> (The Merits of Silence)

36. Iḥyā' Al-Mayyit bi Faḍāil Ahl Al-Bayt <1988> (Giving Life to the Dead with the Merits of the Family of the Prophet ﷺ)

37. Ikhtilāf Al-Madhāhib <1989> (The Divergences Among the Schools of Law)

38. Al-Iklīl fī Istinbāṭ Al-Tanzīl <1981> (The Diadem: The Ex-

traction of Rulings From the Revealed Book)

39. Inbāh Al-Adhkiyā' fī Ḥayāt Al-Anbiyā' <1916> (Notice to the Wise Concerning the Lives of the Prophets)

40. Al-Iqtirāḥ fī 'Ilm Uṣūl Al-Naḥw <1978> (The Authoritative Discourse Concerning the Science of Philology)

41. Al-Izdihār fī mā 'Aqadahu Al-Shu'arā min Al-Aḥādīth wa Al-Āthār <1991> (The Flourishes of Poets Related to the Prophetic Narrations and Sayings of the Companions)

42. Jam' Al-Jawāmi' Al-Ma'rūf bi Al-Jāmi' Al-Kabīr <1970> (The Collection of Collections, Known as the Major Collection)

43. Jami' Al-Aḥādith Al-Jami' Al-Ṣaghīr wa Zawā'idi <1994> (The Minor Collection and Its Addenda)

44. Jany Al-Jinās <1986> (The Genera of Rhetoric)

45. Jazīl Al-Mawāhib fī Ikhtilāf Al-Madhāhib <1992> (The Abundant Gifts Concerning the Differences Among the Schools of Law)

46. Al-Kanz Al-Madfūn wa Al-Falak Al-Mashḥūn <1992> (The Buried Treasure in the Laden Ship: An Encyclopedia of Islamic History)

47. Kashf Al-Ṣalṣala 'an Waṣf Al-Zalzala <1987> (The Transmitted Expositions Concerning the Description of the Earthquake of Doomsday)

48. Al-Radd 'alā Man Akhlada ilā Al-Arḍi wa Jahila Anna Al-Ijtihād fī Kulli 'Aṣrin Farḍ <1984> (Refutation of Those Who Cling to the Earth and Ignore that Scholarly Striving is a Religious Obligation in Every Age)

49. Kitāb Al-Shamārīkh fī 'Ilm Al-Tārīkh <1894> (The Book of Date-Heavy Stalks: A Primer on Historiography)

50. Kitāb Al-Shihāb Al-Thāqib fī Dhamm Al-Khalīl

51. Kitāb Al-Tabarri min Ma'arra Al-Ma'arrī wa Tuḥfa Al-Ẓurafā' bi Asmā' Al-Khulafā'

52. Kitāb Al-Tadhkīr bi Al-Marji' wa Al-Maṣīr

53. Kitāb Asmā' Al-Mudallisīn

54. Kitāb Bughya Al-Wu'ā fī Ṭabaqāt Al-Lughawiyyīn

55. Kitāb Ham' Al-Hawāmi' Sharḥ Jam' Al-Jawāmi' fī 'Ilm Al-Naḥw

56. Kitāb Ḥusn Al-Muḥāḍara fī Akhbār Miṣr wa Al-Qāhira

57. Kitāb Itmām Al-Dirāya li Qurrā' Al-Nuqāya

58. Kitāb Lubb Al-Lubāb fī Taḥrīr Al-Ansāb

59. Tazyīn Al-Mamālik bi Manāqib Imām Mālik

60. Kitāb Tuḥfat Al-Mujalis wa Nuzha Al-Majālis

61. Laqaṭ Al-Marjān fī Aḥkām Al-Jān

62. Lubāb Al-Nuqūl fī Asbāb Al-Nuzūl

63. Al-Luma' fī Khaṣā'is Yawm Al-Jumu'ah

64. Mā Rawāhu Al-Asāṭīn fī 'Adam Al-Majī' ilā Al-Salāṭīn

65. Manāhil Al-Ṣafā Fī Takhrīj Aḥadith Al-Shifā

66. Manāqib Al-Khulafā' Al-Rāshidīn

67. Al-Manhaj Al-Sawī wa Al-Manhal Al-Rawī fī Al-Ṭibb Al-Nabawī

68. Al-Maqāmāt Al-Sundusiyya fī Al-Nisba Al-Muṣṭafawīyya

69. Al-Maṣābīḥ fī Ṣalāt Al-Tarāwīḥ

70. Masālik Al-Ḥunafā' fī Wāliday Al-Muṣṭafā

71. Al-Maṭāli' Al-Sa'īda fī Sharḥ Al-Suyūṭī 'alā Al-Alfiyya Al-Musamma bi Al-Farida fī Al-Naḥw wa Al-Taṣrīf wa Al-Khaṭṭ

72. Maṭla‘ Al-Badrayn fī man Yu’ta Ajrahu Marratayn

73. Miftāḥ Al-Jannah fī Al-I‘tiṣām bi Al-Sunnah

74. Mufḥimāt Al-Aqrān fī Mubhamāt Al-Qur’ān

75. Al-Muhadhdhab fī mā Waqa‘ fī Al-Qur’ān min Al-Mu‘arrab

76. Mu‘jiza Ma‘a Karama fī Kitāb Al-Sharaf Al-Muḥattam: Fī mā Manna Allah Ta‘āla bihi ‘alā Waliyyihi Aḥmad Al-Rifā‘ī

77. Mukhtasar Sharḥ Al-Jāmi‘ Al-Ṣaghīr li Al-Munāwī

78. Muntahā Al-’Āmāl fī Sharḥ Ḥadīth Innama Al-A‘māl

79. Musnad Fātima Al-Zahrā’ Radiya Allah Anha wa mā Warada fī Faḍliha

80. Mustaẓraf min Akhbār Al-Jawārī

81. Mutawakkilī fī mā Warada fī Al-Qur’ān bi Al-Lugha Al-Ḥabashiyya wa Al-Fārisīyya wa Al-Rūmīyya wa Al-Hindīyya wa Al Siryānīyya wa Al-‘Ibrānīyya wa Al-Nabaṭiyya wa Al-Qibṭi-yya wa Al-Turkīyya wa Al-Zanjīyya wa Al-Barbarīyya

82. Nashr Al-‘Alamayn Al-Munīfayn fī Iḥyā’ Al-Abawayn Al-Sharī Fayn

83. Natīja Al-Fikr fī Al-Jahr bi Al-Dhikr

84. Naẓm Al-‘Iqyān fī A‘yān Al-A‘yān

85. Al-Nukat Al-Badī‘āt ‘alā Al-Mawḍū‘āt

86. Nuzha Al-Julasā’ fī Ash’ār Al-Nisā’

87. Nuzha Al-Muta’ammil wa Murshid Al-Muta’ahhil fī Al-Khāṭib wa Al-Mutazawwij

88. Nuzha Al-‘Umr fī Al-Tafḍīl Bayna Al-Bayḍ wa Al-Sumr

89. Nuzul ‘Īsā Ibn Maryam Ākhir Al-Zamān

90. Al-Qawl Al-Jalī fī Faḍā’il ‘Alī

91. Al-Raḥma fī Al-Ṭibb wa Al-Ḥikma

92. Al-Rasā'il Al-'Ashr

93. Raṣf Al-La'āl fī Wasf Al-Hilāl

94. Al-Rawḍ Al-Anīq fī Faḍl Al-Ṣiddīq

95. Risāla Al-Sayf Al-Qāṭi' Al-Lāmi' li Ahl Al-I'tirad Al-Shawa'i'

96. Al-Riyāḍ Al-Anīqa fī Sharḥ Asmā' Khayr Al-Khalīqa Ṣallallāhu 'Alayhi wa Sallam

97. Ṣawn Al-Manṭiq wa Al-Kalām 'an Fann Al-Manṭiq wa Al-Kalām

98. Shaqā'iq Al-Utruj fī Raqā'iq Al-Ghunj

99. Sharḥ Al-Sudūr bi Sharḥ Ḥāl Al-Mawtā wa Al-Qubūr

100. Sharḥ Al-Urjūza Al-Musammā bi 'Uqūd Al-Jumān fī 'Alam Al-Ma'āni wa Al-Bayān

101. Sharḥ Shawāhid Al-Mughnī

102. Shurūṭ Al-Mufassir wa Ādābuh

103. Sihām Al-Iṣāba fī Al-Da'awāt Al-Mujāba

104. Subul Al-Jaliyya fī Al-Ābā' Al-'Aliyya

105. Ta'aqqubāt Al-Suyūṭī 'alā Mawḍū'āt Ibn Al-Jawzī

106. Ṭabaqāt Al-Mufassirīn

107. Tabyīḍ Al-Ṣaḥīfa bi Manaqib Al-Imām Abī Ḥanīfa

108. Al-Tadhyīl wa Al-Tadhnīb 'alā Al-Nihāya fī Gharīb Al-Ḥadīth wa Al-Athar

109. Tadrīb Al-Rāwī fī Sharḥ Taqrīb Al-Nawawī

110. Tahdhīb Al-Khaṣā'iṣ Al-Nabawiyya Al-Kubra

111. Taḥdhīr Al-Khawāṣ min Akādhīb Al-Quṣṣāṣ

112. Takhrīj Aḥādiīth Sharḥ Al-Mawāqif fī 'Ilm Al-Kalām

113. Tamhīd Al-Farsh fī Al-Khiṣāl Al-Mūjiba li Ẓilal Al-ʻArsh

114. Tanbīh Al-Ghabī fī Takhti'a Ibn ʻArabī

115. Tanwīr Al-Ḥawālik Sharḥ ʻala Muwaṭṭa' Mālik

116. Tanwīr Al-Miqbas min Tafsīr Ibn ʻAbbās

117. Tanzīh Al-Anbiyā' ʻan Tashbīh Al-Aghbiyā'

118. Taqrīr Al-Istināḍ fī Tafsīr Al-Ijtihād

119. Al-Taʻrīf bi Ādāb Al-Ta'līf

120. Tārīkh Al-Khulafā'

121. Tartīb Suwar Al-Qur'ān

122. Tasliya Al-Ābā' bi Fuqdān Al-Abnā' Al-Musamma Al-Taʻallul wa Al-Iṭfā' li Nār Lā Tuṭfā'

123. Ṭawq Al-Ḥamāma

124. Ta'yīd Al-Ḥaqīqa Al-ʻAliyya wa Tashyīd Al-Ṭarīqa Al-Shādhiliyya

125. Al-Taʻzīm wa Al-Minna fī Anna Abaway Rasūlallāh fī Al-Jannah

126. Tuḥfa Al-Abrār bi Nukat Al-Adhkār li Al-Nawawī

127. Tuḥfa Al-ʻAjlan fī Faḍā'il ʻUthmān

128. Tuḥfa Al-Nujabā'

129. ʻUqūd Al-Zabarjad ʻalā Musnad Al-Imām Aḥmad

130. ʻUqūd Al-Zabarjad fī Iʻrab Al-Ḥadīth Al-Nabawī

131. Al-Wasā'il fī Musāmara Al-Awā'il

132. Wuṣūl Al-Amānī bi Uṣūl Al-Tahānī

133. Al-Zajr bi Al-Hijr

134. Zubda Al-Laban Fawā'id Lughawiyya wa Ḥadīthīyya

135. Akhlāq Ḥamalat Al-Qur'ān

136. Badhl Al-Himma fī Ṭalab Barā'a Al-Dhimma

137. Al-La'āli' Al-Maṣnū'a fī Al-Aḥādith Al-Mawḍū'a

138. Daqā'iq Al-Akhbār fī Dhikr Al-Jannah wa Al-Nār

139. Al-Itḥāf bi Ḥubb Al-Ashrāf

140. Hay'a Al-Sanīyya fī Al-Hay'a Al-Sunnīyya

Main sources:
Ibn Fahd, *Dhayl Tadhkira Al-Ḥuffāẓ*, pp. 6-10
Al-Suyūṭī, *Tārīkh Al-Khulafā'*, pp. 5-10
Nuh Keller, *Reliance of the Traveller*, p. 1100.

# Towards a Better Du'a

AL-SUYŪṬĪ'S HADITH COMPILATION ON THE RAISING OF HANDS IN DU'A & ADVICE FROM AL-ḤIṢN AL-ḤAṢĪN

Compiled by
**Jalāl al-Dīn al-Suyūṭī**

Translated by
**Talut ibn Sulaiman Dawood**

# 1

# حَدِيث أبي مُوسَى الأَشْعَرِيّ

## HADITH OF ABŪ MŪSĀ AL-ASH'ARĪ

قَالَ البُخَارِيّ فِي الصَّحِيح فِي بَاب الْوضُوء عِنْد الدُّعَاء

١ - حدثنا مُحَمَّد بن الْعَلَاء حدثنا أَبُو أُسَامَة عَن بريد بن عبد الله عَن أبي بردة عَن أبي مُوسَى قَالَ دَعَا النَّبِي صلى الله عَلَيْهِ وَسلم بِمَاء فَتَوَضَّأ بِهِ ثمَّ رفع يَدَيْهِ فَقَالَ اللَّهُمَّ اغْفِر لِعبيد أبي عَامر وَرَأَيْت بَيَاض ابطيه فَقَالَ اللَّهُمَّ اجْعَلْهُ يَوْم الْقِيَامَة فَوق كثير من خلقك من النَّاس. وعلقه البُخَارِيّ فِي بَاب رفع الأَيْدِي فِي الدُّعَاء

Al-Bukhārī said, in his *al-Ṣaḥīḥ,* in the chapter on supplicating before performing ablution:

> Muḥammad ibn al-'Alā' narrated to us that Abū Usāma narrated on the authority of Buraydah ibn 'Abdullāh on the authority of Abī Burdah, who narrated that Abū Mūsā said, 'The Prophet ﷺ supplicated over water and then performed ablution with it. Then he raised his hands and said, "O, Allah! Forgive 'Ubayd Abī 'Āmir. Place him, on the Day of Judgement, over much of the people that You have created."'

Al-Bukhārī also narrated it, without a chain of transmission, in the chapter on raising the hands during supplication.

# حَدِيث أبي هُرَيْرَة

# HADITH OF ABŪ HURAYRAH

## قَالَ البُخَارِيّ فِي الصَّحِيح

٢ - حَدثنَا عَليّ حَدثنَا سُفْيَان أَبُو الزِّنَاد عَن الْأَعْرَج عَن أبي هُرَيْرَة قَالَ قدم الطُّفَيْل بن عَمْرو الدوسي عَليّ رَسُول الله صلى الله عَلَيْهِ وَسلم فَقَالَ يَا رَسُول الله ان دوسا قد عَصَتْ وأبت فَادع الله عَلَيْهَا فَاسْتقْبل الْقبْلَة وَرفع يَدَيْهِ فَظن النَّاس أَنه يَدْعُو عَلَيْهِم فَقَالَ اللَّهُمَّ اهد دوسا وأئت بهم

Al-Bukhārī said in his *al-Ṣaḥīḥ:*

Ali narrated to us that Sufyān Abū al-Zinād narrated on the authority of al-Aʿraj, who narrated that Abū Hurayrah said:

> Ṭufayl ibn ʿAmr al-Dawsī went to the Messenger of Allah ﷺ and said, 'O, Messenger of Allah! [The tribe of] Daws has disobeyed and turned away from Allah. So, supplicate Allah against them.' So he [the Prophet ﷺ] faced the *qiblah* and raised his hands until people believed that he would pray against them but he said, 'O, Allah! Guide Daws and open their hearts to the path of Islam.'

3

## حَدِيث ثَان عَنهُ أبي هُرَيْرَة

## A SECOND HADITH FROM ABŪ HURAYRAH

قَالَ البُخَارِي

٣ - حَدثنَا أَبُو نعيم حَدثنَا الفضيل بن مَرْزُوق عَن عدي بن ثَابت عَن أبي حَازِم عَن أبي هُرَيْرَة رَضِي الله عَنهُ قَالَ ذكر النَّبِي صلى الله عَلَيْهِ وَسلم الرجل يُطِيل السّفر أَشْعَث أغبر يمد يَده الى السَّمَاء يَا رب يَا رب

Al-Bukhārī said:

> Abū Na'īm narrated to us that al-Fuḍayl ibn Marzūq narrated on the authority of 'Adī ibn Thābit who narrated on the authority of Abī Ḥāzim who narrated that Abū Hurayrah *(raḍiyallāhu 'anhu)* said, 'The Prophet ﷺ mentioned a man on a long journey, dishevelled and covered in dust, who stretches his hand towards the sky, saying, "My Lord! My Lord!"'

## حَدِيث ثَالِث عَنهُ

## A THIRD HADITH FROM ABŪ HURAYRAH

قَالَ الْبَزَّار فِي مُسنده

٤ - حَدثنَا مُحَمَّد بن يزِيد حَدثنَا الْمُعْتَمِر عَن أَبِيه عَن بركَة عَن يُشير بن نهيك عَن أبي هُرَيْرَة رَضِي الله عَنهُ قَالَ كَانَ نَبِي الله صلى الله عَلَيْهِ وَسلم يرفع يَده فِي الدُّعَاء حَتَّى يرى بَيَاض ابطيه

قَالَ الْحَافِظ أَبُو الْحسن الهيثمي رِجَاله ثِقَات الا أَن شيخ الْبَزَّار لَا أعرفهُ

Al-Bazzār said, in his *Musnad:*

> Muḥammad ibn Yazīd narrated that al-Muʿtamir narrated from his father on the authority of Barakah who narrated on the authority of Yushīr ibn Nuhayk who narrated that Abū Hurayrah *(raḍiyallāhu ʿanhu)* said, 'The Prophet ﷺ would raise his hands in supplication until the white parts of his underarms were visible.'

Al-Ḥāfiz Abū al-Ḥasan al-Haythamī said, 'Its narrators are all trustworthy, except the sheikh of al-Bazzār. I do not know him.'

# 5

## حَدِيث ابْن عمر

## HADITH OF IBN ʿUMAR

قَالَ الْبُخَارِيّ فِي الْأَدَب الْمُفْرد

٥ - حَدثنَا ابراهيم بن الْمُنْذر حَدثنَا ابْن فليح أخبرنَا أبي عَن أبي نعيم وَهُوَ وهب قَالَ رَأَيْت ابْن عمر وَابْن الزبير يديران الراحتين على الْوَجْه

وَبَوَّبَ عَلَيْهِ بَاب رفع الْأَيْدِي فِي الدُّعَاء

Al-Bukhārī said, in *Kitāb al-Adab al-Mufrad,* ʿIbrāhīm ibn Mundhir narrated to us that Ibn Fulayḥ narrated that his father related to him, that Abū Naʿīm, whose name is Wahb, said, "I saw Ibn ʿUmar and Ibn al-Zubayr wiping their palms over their face [after supplication].'"

Al-Bukhārī placed it in the chapter on raising hands during supplication.

# 6

## حَدِيث أنس رضى الله عَنهُ

## HADITH OF ANAS *(RAḌIYALLĀHU ʿANHU)*

أخرجه البُخَارِيّ فِي الصَّحِيح قَالَ

٦ - وَقَالَ الأويسي حَدثنِي مُحَمَّد بن جَعْفَر عَن يحيى بن سعيد وَشريك سمعا أنسا عَن النَّبِي صلى الله عَلَيْهِ وَسلم أَنه رفع يَدَيْهِ حَتَّى رَأَيْت بَيَاض ابطيه

Al-Bukhārī narrated the following in his *al-Ṣaḥīḥ:* ʻAl-Uways said that Muḥammad ibn Jaʿfar narrated that both Yaḥyā bin Saʿīd and Shurayk heard from Anas that the Prophet ﷺ raised his hands until the white parts of his underarms were visible.

# 7

## حَدِيث ثَان عَنهُ

## A SECOND HADITH OF ANAS

٧ - قَالَ أَبُو دَاوُد فِي السّنَن

حَدثنَا عقبَة بن مكرم حَدثنَا مُسلم بن قُتَيْبَة عَن عمر بن نَبهَان عَن قَتَادَة عَن أنس قَالَ رَأَيْت رَسُول الله يَدْعُو هَكَذَا بباطن كفيه وظاهرهما

Abū Dāwūd said, in his *Sunan:* "ʿAqabah ibn Mukarram narrated that Muslim ibn Qutaybah narrated, on the authority of ʿUmar ibn Nabahān, that Qatādah narrated that Anas said, "I saw the Messenger of Allah supplicate in this way, with both the palms and the backs of his hands.""

# 8

## حَدِيث ثَالِث عَنهُ

## A THIRD HADITH OF ANAS

قَالَ الْبَزَّار

٨ - أخبرنَا أَحْمد بن يحيي حَدثنَا عمر بن حَفْص حَدثنَا أبي عَن الْأَعْمَش ح
قَالَ الطَّبَرَانِيّ فِي الْأَوْسَط

حَدثنَا مُحَمَّد بن عبد الله الْحَضْرَمِيّ حَدثنَا عَليّ بن اسحق السَّمرقَنْدِي حَدثنَا الْفضل بن مُوسَى الشَّيْبَانِيّ عَن الْأَعْمَش عَن أنس بن مَالك رَضِي الله عَنهُ قَالَ رفع رَسُول الله صلى الله عَلَيْهِ وَسلم يَدَيْهِ بِعَرَفَة يَدْعُو فَقَالَ أَصْحَاب النَّبِي صلى الله عَلَيْهِ وَسلم هَذَا الابتهال ثمَّ جالت النَّاقة فَفتح احدى يَدَيْهِ فَأَخذهَا وَهُوَ رَافع الْأُخْرَى

رجال الْبَزَّار رجال الصَّحِيح وَهُوَ ثِقَة لَكِن الْأَعْمَش لم يسمع عَن أنس

Al-Bazzār said:

Aḥmad ibn Yaḥyā informed us that ʿUmar ibn Hafṣ narrated to him that his father narrated, on the authority of al-Aʿmash, and that al-Ṭabarānī said in his *Awsaṭ:*

> Muḥammad ibn ʿAbdullāh al-Ḥaḍramī narrated that ʿAlī ibn Isḥāq al-Samarqandī narrated to him that al-Faḍl ibn Mūsā al-Shaybānī narrated on the authority

of al-Aʿmash that Anas ibn Malik (*raḍiyallāhu ʿanhu*) said, 'The Messenger of Allah ﷺ raised his hands in supplication at ʿArafah. The Companions of the Prophet ﷺ said, "He is supplicating." Then, his she-camel started to walk off. So, he reached out with one of his hands and restrained her while he was raising the other.'

Al-Bazzār's narrators are the men of *ṣaḥīḥ* traditions. And, he is trustworthy. However, al-Aʿmash never heard hadiths from Anas.

## حَدِيث رَابع عَنهُ

## A FOURTH HADITH OF ANAS

9

قَالَ أَبُو نعيم فِي الْحِلْية

٩ - حَدثنَا سُلَيْمَان بن أَحْمد حَدثنَا الْمِقْدَام بن دَاوُد حَدثنَا حبيب بن أبي حبيب حَدثنَا هِشَام بن سعيد عَن ربيعَة بن أبي عبد الرَّحْمَن قَالَ سَمِعت أنس بن مَالك يَقُول قَالَ رَسُول الله صلى الله عَلَيْهِ وَسلم ان الله جواد كريم يستحي من العَبْد الْمُسلم اذا دَعَاهُ أَن يرد يَدَيْهِ صفرا لَيْسَ فيهمَا شَيْء فاذا دَعَا العَبْد وَأَشَارَ باصبعه قَالَ الرب جلّ وَعلا أخْلص عَبدِي واذا رفع يَدَيْهِ قَالَ الله تَعَالَى اني أستحي من عَبدِي أَن أرده

Abū Na'īm said in his *Ḥilyah:* Sulayman ibn Aḥmad narrated to us that al-Miqdām ibn Dāwūd narrated to him that Ḥabīb ibn Abī Ḥabīb narrated to him that Hishām ibn Sa'īd narrated that Rabī'ah ibn Abī 'Abd al-Raḥmān said:

> I heard Anas ibn Mālik saying, 'The Messenger of Allah ﷺ said, "Indeed, Allah is Openhanded and extremely Generous. He is too shy towards a Muslim servant who calls upon him that he should leave his hands empty, having nothing in them. So, when the servant supplicates, pointing with his finger, the Lord *(subḥānahu wa ta 'ālā)* says, 'My slave has made his worship exclusively for Me.' And when he raises his hands, Allah *(ta 'ālā)* says, 'I am too bashful toward My slave to reject him.'"'

10

# حَدِيث خَامِس عَنهُ

# A FIFTH HADITH OF ANAS

قَالَ عبد الرَّزَّاق

١٠ - أخبرنَا معمر عَن أبان عَن أنس قَالَ قَالَ رَسُول الله صلى الله عَلَيْهِ وَسلم أَن ربكُم حيي كريم يستحي اذا رفع العَبْد يَدَيْهِ اليه أَن يردهما صفرا حَتَّى يَجْعَل فيهمَا خيرا

ʿAbd al-Razzāq said:

'Muʿammar informed us on the authority of Abān that Anas said, "The Messenger of Allah ﷺ said, 'Indeed, your Lord is Bashful and Noble. He becomes too bashful when a servant raises his hands to leave them empty and not fill them with good.'"'

11

# وَقَالَ الْخَطِيب فِي الْمُتَّفق والمفترق

## AL-KHAṬĪB SAID IN *AL-MUTTAFAQ WA AL-MUFATARAQ:*

١١ - أخبرنَا القَاضِي أَبُو بكر أَحْمد بن الْحسن الْحَرَشِي حَدثنَا أَبُو الْعَبَّاس مُحَمَّد بن يَعْقُوب الْأَصَم حَدثنَا مُحَمَّد بن اسحاق الصَّنْعَانِيّ حَدثنَا مُحَمَّد بن أَحْمد حَدثنَا ابراهيم بن الْمُخْتَار حَدثنَا ابْن جريج عَن أبان بن عُثْمَان عَن أنس بن مَالك أَن رَسُول الله كَانَ يرفع يَدَيْهِ عِنْد الابتهال هَكَذَا

Qāḍī Abū Bakr Aḥmad ibn al-Ḥasan al-Ḥarashī informed us that Abū al-ʿAbbās Muḥammad ibn Yaʿqūb al-Aṣam narrated to him that Muḥammad ibn Isḥāq al-Ṣanʿānī narrated to him that Muḥammad ibn Aḥmad narrated to him that Ibrāhīm ibn al-Mukhtār narrated to him that Ibn Jurayj narrated on the authority of Abān ibn ʿUthmān that Anas ibn Mālik narrated that the Messenger of Allah ﷺ used to raise his hands whenever he supplicated.

# 12

# حَدِيث عمر بن الْخطاب رضى الله عَنهُ

# A HADITH OF ʿUMAR IBN AL-KHAṬṬĀB (*RAḌIYALLĀHU ʿANHU*)

قَالَ التِّرْمِذِيّ

١٢ - حَدثنَا أَبُو مُوسَى مُحَمَّد بن الْمثنى وابراهيم بن يَعْقُوب وَغير وَاحِد قَالُوا حَدثنَا حَمَّاد بن عِيسَى الْجُهَنِيّ عَن حَنْظَلَة بن أبي سُفْيَان الجُمَحِي عَن سَالم بن عبد الله عَن أَبِيه عَن عمر بن الْخطاب رَضِي الله عَنهُ قَالَ كَانَ رَسُول الله صلى الله عَلَيْهِ وَسلم اذا رفع يَدَيْهِ فِي الدُّعَاء لم يحطهما حَتَّى يمسح بهما وَجهه

رِجَاله رجال الصَّحِيح سوى حَمَّاد وَهُوَ شيخ صَالح ضَعِيف الحَدِيث ولحديثه هَذَا شَوَاهِد فَهُوَ حسن وَفِي بعض نسخ التِّرْمِذِيّ أَنه قَالَ فِيهِ صَحِيح

Al-Tirmidhī said:

> Abū Mūsā Muḥammad ibn al-Muthanna, Ibrāhīm ibn Yaʿqūb and others narrated to us saying, Ḥammād ibn ʿĪsā al-Juhanī narrated to us, on the authority of Hanẓalah ibn Abī Sufyān al-Jumaḥī who said, on the authority of ʿAbdullāh from his father that ʿUmar ibn al-Khaṭṭāb *(raḍiyallāhu ʿanhu)* said, 'The Messenger of Allah ﷺ used to raise his hands during supplication and would not put them down until he had wiped them both over his face.'

ts narrators are people of *ṣaḥīḥ* traditions, except for Ḥammād. He was a pious sheikh but was weak in Hadith. However, this hadith has supporting evidences so its grade is *ḥasan*. In some of the manuscripts of al-Tirmidhī, the author said that it is authentic *(ṣaḥīḥ)*.

# 13

## أثر أبي بكر الصّديق رَضِي الله عَنهُ

## A NARRATION ON ABU BAKR AL-ṢIDDĪQ *(RAḌIYALLĀHU ʿANHU)*

قَالَ ابْن عَسَاكِر

١٣ - أخبرنَا أَبُو الْقَاسِم السَّمرقَنْدِي أخبرنَا أَبُو عَليّ مُحَمَّد بن أَحْمد الصَّواف أخبرنَا الْحسن بن عَليّ الْقطَّان حَدثنَا اسماعيل بن عِيسَى الْعَطَّار أحبرنا أَبُو حُذَيْفَة اسحق بن بشر عَمَّن ذكره قَالَ

بعث أَبُو بكر سعيد بن عَامر بن حذيم وَأمره أَن يسير حَتَّى يلْحق بِيَزِيد بن أبي سُفْيَان فَقَالَ أَبُو بكر عباد الله ادعوا الله أَن يصحب صَاحبكُم واخوانكم مَعَه ويسلمهم فارفعوا أَيْدِيكُم رحمكم الله أَجْمَعِينَ فَرفع الْقَوْم أَيْديهم وهم أَكثر من خمسين وَقَالَ عَليّ مَا رفع عدَّة من الْمُسلمين أَيْديهم يسألونه شَيْئا الا اسْتُجَاب لَهُم مَا لم يكن مَعْصِيّة أَو قطيعة رحم

Ibn ʿAsākir said: Abū al-Qāsim al-Samarqandī informed us that Abū ʿAlī Muhamamd ibn Aḥmad al-Ṣawāf informed him that al-Ḥasan ibn ʿAlī al-Qaṭṭān informed him that Ismāʿīl ibn ʿĪsā al-ʿAṭṭār narrated to him that Abū Ḥudhayfah Isḥāq ibn Bishr had informed him on the authority of someone who mentioned:

> Abu Bakr sent Saʿīd ibn ʿĀmir ibn Ḥudhaym on an expedition, ordering him to travel until he met Yazīd

ibn Abī Sufyān. Abu Bakr said, 'Servants of Allah! Ask Allah that He accompany your companion and your brothers who are with him, and that He keeps them safe. And raise your hands. May Allah have mercy on you all.' There were more than fifty people and they all raised their hands. Ali said, 'No group of Muslims raise their hands asking Allah for something except that He responds to them, as long as they do not seek something that entails disobedience or severing of ties.'

# 14

## اثر عمر بن الخطاب رَضِي اللهُ عَنهُ

## A NARRATION ON ʿUMAR IBN AL-KHAṬṬĀB (*RAḌIYALLĀHU ʿANHU*)

قَالَ ابْن عَساكِر

١٤ - أخبرنَا أَبُو نصر غَالب بن أَحْمد الْمُسلم حَدثنَا أَبُو الْقَاسِم مكي ابْن عبد السَّلَام بن الْحُسَيْن الْمَقْدِسِي أخبرنَا أَبُو مُحَمَّد عبد الْعَزِيز بن أَحْمد النصيبي أخبرنَا أَبُو الْفَتْح مُحَمَّد بن ابراهيم بن مُحَمَّد بن يزِيد الْبَصْرِيّ أخبرنَا سعيد بن عبد الرَّحْمَن بن أبي العمياء عَن السَّائِب ابْن خباب أَن أَبَا بكر توفّي واستخلف عمر بن الْخطاب رَضِي الله عنه فَقَالَ أهل الشَّام فظ غليظ شَدِيد مَا هُوَ لطى بملائم وكرهوا خِلَافَته فَبلغ عمر فَرفع يَدَيْهِ فَقَالَ اللَّهُمَّ حببهم الي وحببني اليهم

Ibn ʿAsākir said:

Abū Naṣr Ghālib ibn Aḥmad al-Muslim informed us that Abū Qāsim Makkī ibn ʿAbd al-Salām ibn al-Ḥusayn al-Maqdisī narrated to us that Abū Muḥammad ʿAbd al-ʿAzīz ibn Aḥmad al-Naṣībī informed him that Abū al-Fatḥ Muḥammad ibn Ibrāhīm ibn Muḥammad ibn Yazīd al-Baṣarī informed him that Saʿīd ibn ʿAbd al-Raḥmān ibn Abī al-ʿUmyā' informed him on the authority of al-Sā'ib ibn Khabāb that Abu Bakr passed away and ʿUmar ibn al-Khaṭṭāb *(raḍiyallāhu ʿanhu)* succeeded him. The people of Sham began to say that he was extremely harsh hearted and that he was not fit for the position. And, they disliked his succession. That news reached Umar so he raised his hands and said, 'O, Allah! Make me love them and make them love me.'

15

## حَدِيث ثَان عَنهُ

## A SECOND HADITH FROM UMAR

قَالَ مُسلم فِي الصَّحِيح

١٥ - حَدثنَا هناد بن السّري حَدثنَا ابْن الْمُبَارك عَن عِكْرِمَة بن عمار ح وَقَالَ التِّرْمِذِيّ حَدثنَا مُحَمَّد بن بشار حَدثنَا عمر بن يُونُس اليامي قَالَ حَدثنَا عِكْرِمَة بن عمار حَدثنَا أَبُو زميل حَدثنَا عبد الله بن عَبَّاس حَدثنِي عمر بن الْخطاب قَالَ

نظر نَبِي الله صلى الله عَلَيْهِ وَسلم وهم الف وَأَصْحَابه ثَلَاثمِائَة وَبضْعَة عشر رجَالًا فَاسْتقْبل الْقبْلَة وَمد يَدَيْهِ وَجعل يَهْتِف بربه اللَّهُمَّ أَنْجز لي مَا وَعَدتنِي اللَّهُمَّ ان تهْلك هَذِه الْعِصَابَة من أهل الاسلام لَا تعبد فِي الأَرْض فَمَا زَالَ يَهْتِف بربه مَادًّا يَدَيْهِ مُسْتَقْبلا الْقبْلَة حَتَّى سقط رِدَاءَهُ عَن مَنْكِبَيْهِ

Muslim said in his *al-Ṣaḥīḥ,* 'Hanād ibn al-Sarī narrated to us that Ibn al-Mubārak narrated to him, on the authority of 'Ikrimah ibn 'Ammār.'

And al-Tirmidhī said:

Muḥammad ibn Bashshar narrated to us that 'Umar ibn Yūnus al-Yāmī narrated saying, 'Ikrima ibn 'Ammār narrated to us that Abū Zamīl narrated to him that 'Abdullāh ibn 'Abbās narrated that 'Umar ibn al-Khaṭṭāb said:

15

The Prophet ﷺ looked and they were a thousand men while his companions were a little over 310. So, he turned towards the *qiblah,* spread his hands and began to speak with his Lord, *'O, Allah! Deliver to me what You have promised me. O, Allah! If You allow this small band of the people of Islam to perish, You will not be worshiped on the face of the Earth.'* He continued to speak to his Lord, with his hands out spread, facing the *qiblah,* until his garment slipped from his shoulders.

# 16

## حَدِيث ثَالِث عَنهُ

## A THIRD HADITH FROM UMAR

قَالَ التِّرمِذِيّ

١٦ - حَدثنَا يحي بن مُوسَى وَعبد بن حميد وَغير وَاحِد قَالُوا حَدثنَا عبد الرَّزَّاق عَن يُونُس بن سليم عَن االزهري عَن عُروَة بن الزبير عَن عبد الرَّحْمَن بن عبد الْقَارِي قَالَ سَمِعت عمر بن الْخطاب يَقُول

كَانَ رَسُول الله صلى الله عَلَيْهِ وَسلم اذا نزل عَلَيْهِ الْوَحْي سمع عِنْد وَجهه كَدوِيّ النَّحل فَأنْزل عَلَيْهِ يَوْمًا فَمَكَثْنَا سَاعَة فسرِّي عَنهُ فَاسْتقْبل الْقبْلَة وَرفع يَدَيْهِ وَقَالَ اللَّهُمَّ زِدْنَا وَلَا تنْقصنَا وَأَكْرمنَا لَا تهنا وَأَعْطِنَا وَلَا تحْرِمنَا وَآثرنَا وَلَا تُؤثر علينا وَأَرْضنَا وَارْضَ عَنَّا

أخرجه الْحَاكِم فِي الْمُسْتَدْرك وَقَالَ صَحِيح السناد

Al-Tirmidhī said:

Yaḥyā ibn Mūsā, ʿAbd ibn Ḥamīd, and others narrated to me that ʿAbd al-Razzāq from Yūnus ibn Sulaym, from al-Zuhrī, from ʿUrwah ibn al-Zubayr that ʿAbd al-Raḥmān ibn ʿAbd al-Qārī said:

I heard ʿUmar ibn al-Khaṭṭāb say, 'Whenever revelation would descend on the Messenger of Allah ﷺ, one would hear, near his face, a sound similar to the buzzing of bees. One day, it descended upon him and we remained for an hour. Then, it was lifted from him. And he faced the *qiblah* and raised his hands, saying, "O, Allah! Increase us and do not decrease us. Honour us and do not lower us. Grant us [good] and do not withhold from us. Prefer us and do not prefer anyone over us. Make us pleased and be pleased with us.'"

*Al-Ḥākim* narrated it in his Mustadrak and said its chain of narration is authentic [*ṣaḥīḥ*].

# 17 حَدِيث عَلِيّ بن أَبِي طَالب رَضِي الله عَنهُ

# A HADITH OF ʿALĪ IBN ABĪ ṬĀLIB *(RAḌIYALLĀHU ʿANHU)*

قَالَ البُخَارِيّ

١٧ - حَدثنَا مُسلم حَدثنَا عبد الله بن دَاوُد عَن نعيم بن حَكِيم عَن أبي مَرْيَم عَن عَليّ رَضِي الله عَنهُ قَالَ رفع رَسُول الله صلى الله عَلَيْهِ وَسلم يَدَيْهِ وَقَالَ اللَّهُمَّ عَلَيْك بالوليد

Al-Bukhārī said:

Muslim narrated to us that ʿAbdullāh ibn Dāwūd narrated to him, on the authority of Naʿīm ibn Ḥakīm, on the authority of Abī Maryam, that Ali *(raḍiyallāhu ʿanhu)* said, 'The Messenger of Allah ﷺ raised his hands and said, "O, Allah! Take care of Walīd."'

# 18

## حَدِيث عَائِشَة رَضِي الله عَنْهَا

## A HADITH FROM ʿĀ'ISHAH

### قَالَ البُخَارِيّ فِي كتاب رفع الْيَدَيْنِ فِي الصَّلَاة

١٨ - حَدثنَا يحي بن مُوسَى حَدثنَا عبد الحميد حَدثنَا اسماعيل بن عبد الْملك عَن ابْن أبي مليكَة عَن عَائِشَة قَالَت رَأَيْت النَّبِي صلى الله عَلَيْهِ وَسلم رَافعا يَدَيْهِ حَتَّى بدا ضبعيه يَدْعُو

Al-Bukhārī said in *The Book on Raising One's Hand in Prayer*: Yaḥyā ibn Mūsā narrated to us that ʿAbd al-Ḥamīd narrated to him that Ismāʿīl ibn ʿAbd al-Malik narrated on the authority of Abī Malīkah that ʿĀ'ishah said, 'I saw the Prophet ﷺ raise his hands until his upper arms became visible and supplicate.'

# 19

## حَدِيث ثَان عَنْهَا

## A SECOND HADITH FROM ʿĀ'ISHAH

وَقَالَ فِيهِ

١٩ - حَدثنَا مُسَدّد حَدثنَا أَبُو عوَانَة عَن سماك بن حَرْب عَن عِكْرِمَة عَن عَائِشَة رَضِي الله عَنْهَا يزْعم أَنه سَمعه مِنْهَا أَنَّهَا رَأَتْ النَّبِي صلى الله عَلَيْهِ وَسلم يَدْعُو رَافعا يَدَيْهِ يَقُول اللَّهُمَّ انما أَنا بشر فَلَا تعاقبني أَيّمَا رجل من الْمُؤمنِينَ آذيته وشتمته فَلَا تعاقبني فِيهِ

وَقَالَ عبد الرازق فِي الْمُصَنّف

عَن اسرائيل بن يُونُس عَن سماك بن حَرْب عَن عِكْرِمَة عَن عَائِشَة رَضِي الله عَنْهَا قَالَت كَانَ رَسُول الله صلى الله عَلَيْهِ وَسلم يرفع يَدَيْهِ حَتَّى أَنِّي لأسأم لَهُ مِمَّا يرفعها اللَّهُمَّ انما أَنا بشر فَلَا تعذبني بهم رجل شتمته أَو آذيته

Al-Bukhārī also narrated in the same place (*The Book on Raising One's Hand in Prayer*):

Musadad narrated to us that Abū ʿAwānah narrated to him on the authority of Samāk ibn Ḥarb on the authority of ʿIkrimah that ʿĀ'ishah *(raḍiyallāhu ʿanhā)*, and it is believed that he heard it directly from her, saw the Prophet ﷺ supplicating while raising his hands, saying, "O, Allah! I am only a human being. So, do not take me to task. If I harm or insult a believing person, don't take me to task."

Isrā'īl ibn Yūnus narrated on the authority of Samak ibn Harb on the authority of ʿIkrimah that ʿĀ'ishah (*raḍiyallāhu ʿanhā)* said, 'The Messenger of Allah ﷺ used to raise his hands until I became impatient with how long he had them raised, [saying], "O, Allah! I am only a man. So do not punish me for any man that I have insulted or harmed."'

# 20

# حَدِيث ثَالِث عَنْهَا

## A THIRD HADITH FROM ʿĀʾISHAH

وَقَالَ فِيهِ

٢٠ - حَدثنَا قُتَيْبَة حَدثنَا عبد الْعَزِيز بن مُحَمَّد عَن عَلْقَمَة بن أبي عَلْقَمَة عَن أَبِيه عَن عَائِشَة قَالَت خرج رَسُول الله صلى الله عَلَيْهِ وَسلم ذَات لَيْلَة فَأرْسلت بَرِيرَة فِي أَثَره تنظر أَيْن يذهب فسلك نَحْو بَقِيع الْغَرْقَد فَوقف فِي وَادي البقيع فَرفع يَدَيْهِ ثمَّ انْصَرف فَرَجَعت بَرِيرَة فأخبرتني فَلَمَّا أَصبَحت سَأَلته فَقلت يَا رَسُول الله أَيْن خرجت اللَّيْلَة قَالَ بعثت الي أهل البقيع لأصلي عَلَيْهِم

He also narrated in the same place:

Qutaybah narrated to us that ʿAbd al-ʿAzīz ibn Muḥammad narrated on the authority of ʿAlqamah ibn Abī ʿAlqamah, who narrated on the authority of his father, that ʿĀʾishah said:

> The Messenger of Allah ﷺ left one night. So, I sent Barīrah behind him to see where he had gone. He travelled toward Baqīʿ. He stopped in the valley of Baqīʿ and raised his hands. Then, he went off and Barīrah returned and informed me. When I awoke, I asked him, 'O, Messenger of Allah! Where did you go last night?' He replied, 'I was sent to the people of Baqīʿ to pray over them.'

## حَدِيث رَابع عَنْهَا

## 21 A FOURTH HADITH FROM ʿĀʾISHAH

قَالَ الامام أَحْمد فِي مُسْنده

٢١ - حَدثنَا الْحجَّاج قَالَ أَنا ابْن جريج قَالَ حَدثنِي عبد الله رجل من قُرَيْش أَنه سمع مُحَمَّد بن قيس بن مخرمَة بن الْمطلب أَنه قَالَ يَوْمًا أَلا أحدثكُم عني وَعَن أُمِّي فظننا أَنه يُرِيد أمه الَّتِي وَلدته قَالَت عَائِشَة أَلا أحدثكُم عني وَعَن رَسُول الله صلى الله عَلَيْهِ وَسلم قلت بلَى قَالَ قَالَت لما كَانَت لَيْلَتي الَّتِي النَّبِي فِيهَا عِنْدِي انْقَلب فَوضع رِدَاء وخلع نَعْلَيْه فوضعهما عِنْد رجلَيْهِ وَبسط طرف ازاره على فرَاشه فاضطجع فَلم يلبث الا ريثما ظن أَنِّي قد رقدت فَأخذ رِدَاءَهُ رويدا وانتعل رويدا وَفتح الْبَاب فَخرج ثمَّ أجافه رويدا فَجعلت دِرعِي فِي راسي واختمرت وتقنعت ازاري ثمَّ انْطَلَقت على أَثَره حَتَّى جَاءَ البقيع فَقَامَ فَأطَال الْقيام ثمَّ رفع يَدَيْهِ ثَلَاث مَرَّات ثمَّ انحرف فانحرفت فأسرع فأسرعت فهرول فهرولت فأحضر فأحضرت فسبقته

فَدخلت فَلَيْسَ الا أَن اضطجعت فَدخل فَقَالَ مَالك يَا عائش حشيا رابية قَالَت قلت لَا شَيْء يَا رَسُول الله قَالَ لتخبرينني أَو ليخبرني اللَّطِيف الْخَبِير قَالَت قلت يَا رَسُول الله بِأبي أَنْت وَأمي فَأَخْبَرته قَالَ فَأَنت السوَاد الَّذِي رَأَيْت أَمَامِي قلت نعم فلهزني فِي ظَهْرِي لهزة فأوجعني وَقَالَ أظننت أَن يَحِيف عَلَيْك الله وَرَسُوله قَالَت مهما تكتم النَّاس يُعلمهُ الله قَالَ نعم فان جِبْرِيل عَلَيْهِ السَّلَام أَتَانِي حِين رَأَيْت فناداني فأخفاه مِنْك فأجبته

خفيته مِنْك وَلم يكن ليدْخل عَلَيْك وَقد وضعت ثِيَابك وظننت أَنَّك قد
رقدت فَكرِهت أَن أوقظك وخشيت أَن تستوخشي فَقَالَ ان رَبك جلّ
وَعز يأامرك أَن تَأْتي أهل البقيع فتستغفر لَهُم قَالَت فَكيف أَقُول يَا رَسُول
الله قَالَ قولي السَّلَام على أهل الديار من الْمُؤمنِينَ وَالْمُسْلِمين وَيرْحَم الله
الْمُسْتَقْدِمِينَ منا والمستأخرين وانا ان شَاءَ الله للاحقون

Imam Aḥmad said, in his *Musnad:*

Al-Ḥajjāj narrated to us saying, 'I am Ibn Jurayḥ. ʿAbdullāh, a man of Quraysh, narrated to me that he heard Muḥammad ibn Qays ibn Makhramah ibn al-Muṭṭalib one day say, "Should I not narrate to you something from my mother?" I (ʿAbdullāh) assumed that he was speaking about the mother that bore him. ʿĀ'ishah said, 'Should I not narrate to something about me and the Messenger of Allah ﷺ?' I said, 'Of course'. So, she said:

> Once, when the two nights that the Prophet would spend with me came, he arrived, took off his robe and sandals and placed them at his feet. He then spread the ends of his lower garment over his mattress and laid down. However, he only stayed until he assumed that I had fallen asleep. Then he gently grabbed his garment, gently put on his sandals, opened the door, exited and then closed it behind him gently. So I put my outer garment over my head, put on my head scarf, and covered my face with my lower garment. I then followed his footsteps until he came to Baqīʿ. He

stood there for a long time. Then, he raised his hands three times. Then, he turned around and I turned back. He started to walk quickly and so did I. He ran and I ran until we arrived home. I arrived before him and entered. Just as I was going to lay down, he entered and said, 'O, 'Ā'ishah! Why are you breathing so heavily?' I said, 'No reason, O, Messenger of Allah.' he said, 'Either you will inform me, or the Most Subtle will.' I said, 'O, Messenger of Allah! My mother and father be sacrificed for you.' And I informed him of what had happened. He said, 'So, you were the shadow that I saw?' I said, 'Yes'. He nudged me in my back until I felt some pain and said, 'Do you think that Allah and His Messenger would be unjust with you?' I said, 'Whatever people hide, Allah still knows it.' He said, 'Certainly. Jibrīl (*'alayhi al-salām)* came to me when you saw me. He called me and I hid that from you. I answered him in a way that was hidden from you. And, he would not have entered upon you after you had taken off your clothes. I thought you had fallen asleep so I didn't want to wake you and I feared I may frighten you. Your Lord *('azza wa jall)* has ordered you to come to the people of Baqī' and seek forgiveness for them.' I said, 'What should I say, O, Messenger of Allah?' He replied, 'Say: O, people of the abode of the believers and the Muslims! May Allah have mercy on you, both those that preceded us and those that will follow us. And we, if Allah so wills, will soon join you.'

# 22

## حَدِيث سلمَان رَضِي الله عَنهُ

## A HADITH OF SALMĀN *(RAḌIYALLĀHU ʿANHU)*

قَالَ أَبُو دَاوُد

٢٢ - حَدثنَا مُؤَمل بن الْفضل الْحَرَّانِي حَدثنَا عِيسَى بن يُونُس حَدثنَا جَعْفَر يَعْنِي ابْن مَيْمُون صَاحب الأنماط حَدثنَا أَبُو عُثْمَان عَن سلمَان قَالَ قَالَ رَسُول الله صلى الله عَلَيْهِ وَسلم ان ربكُم حييّ كَرِيم يستحي من عَبده اذا رفع يَدَيْهِ اليه أَن يردهما صفرا. أخرجه التِّرْمِذِيّ وَابْن مَاجَه قَالَ التِّرْمِذِيّ حسن وَقد تَابعه مُحَمَّد بن الزبْرِقَان عَن سُلَيْمَان اليمي عَن أبي عُثْمَان

Abū Dāwūd said:

> Mu'ammal ibn al-Faḍl al-Ḥarrānī narrated to us that ʿĪsā ibn Yūnus narrated to him that Jaʿfar, meaning Ibn Maymūn the stamp seller, narrated to him that Abū ʿUthmān narrated that Salmān said, 'The Messenger of Allah ﷺ said, "Your Lord is very Bashful and Generous. He is too bashful of His slave that He should, when he raises his hands, leave them empty."'

Al-Tirmidhī and Ibn Mājah narrated it. Al-Tirmidhī said that it is a *ḥasan* hadith. Muḥammad ibn al-Zubriqān corroborated this hadith from Sulaymān al-Yammī on the authority of Abū ʿUthmān.

# 23

## حَدِيث ثَان عَنهُ

## A SECOND HADITH OF SALMĀN

٢٣ - حَدثنَا يَعْقُوب بن مُجَاهِد الْبَصْرِيّ عَن الْمُنْذر بن الْوَلِيد الجارودي عَن أَبِيه عَن شَدَّاد أبي طَلْحَة الرَّاسِبِي عَن الْجريرِي عَن أبي عُثْمَان عَن سلمَان قَالَ قَالَ رَسُول الله صلى الله عَلَيْهِ وَسلم مَا رفع قوم أكفهم الى الله عز وَجل يسألونه شَيْء الا كَانَ حَقًا على الله أَن يضع فِي أَيْديهم الَّذِي يسألونه

رِجَاله رجال الصَّحِيح

Yaʿqūb ibn Mujāhid al-Baṣarī narrated to us from al-Mundhir ibn al-Wālid al-Jārūdī from his father from Shaddād ibn Abī Ṭalḥah al-Rasibī from al-Jarīrī from Abū ʿUthmān that Salmān said, 'The Messenger of Allah ﷺ said, "No people raise the palms of their hands to Allah (*ʿazza wa jall)* requesting something of Him, except that it becomes incumbent upon Allah to place that which they have asked in their hands."'

Its narrators are men of authentic traditions.

24

# حَدِيث مَالك بن يَسَار

# HADITH MĀLIK IBN YASĀR

٢٤ - حَدثنَا سُلَيْمَان بن عبد الحميد البهراني قَالَ قرأته فِي أصل اسماعيل يَعْنِي ابْن عَيَّاش

حَدثنِي ضَمْضَم عَن شُرَيْح حَدثنَا أَبُو ظَبْيَة أَن أَبَا بحرية السكونِي حَدثهُ عَن مَالك بن يَسَار السكونِي ثمَّ الْعَوْفِيّ وَله صُحْبَة أَن رَسُول الله صلى الله عَلَيْهِ وَسلم قَالَ اذا سالتم الله فَاسْأَلُوهُ ببطون أكفكم وَلَا تسألوه بظهورها

Sulaymān ibn ʿAbd al-Ḥamīd al-Baharānī narrated to us, saying, 'I read the following in the original manuscript of Ismāʿīl ibn ʿAyyāsh:

> Ḍamḍam narrated to me that Shurayḥ said that Abū Ẓabya narrated to him that Abū Bariyyah al-Sukūnī narrated to him that Mālik ibn Yasār al-Sukūnī al-ʿAwfī, who was a companion, narrated that the Messenger of Allah ﷺ said, "Whenever you ask Allah for something, ask him with the palms of your hands. Don't ask him with the backs of your hands."'

25

## حَدِيث جَابر رَضِي اللهُ عَنهُ

## HADITH JĀBIR (*RAḌIYALLĀHU ʿANHU*)

قَالَ البُخَارِيّ فِي الْأَدَب الْمُفْرد فِي كِتَاب رفع الْيَدَيْنِ فِي الصَّلَاة

٢٥ - حَدثنَا حَمَّاد بن زيد حَدثنَا حجاج الصَّواف عَن أبي الزبير عَن جَابر بن عبد الله أَن الطُّفَيْل بن عَمْرو قَالَ للنَّبِي هَل لَك فِي حصن ومنعة حصن دوس قَالَ فَأبى رَسُول الله صلى الله عَلَيْهِ وَسلم لما ادخر الله الْأَنْصَار فَهَاجر الطُّفَيْل وَهَاجَر مَعَه رجل من قومه فَمَرض الرجل فضجر وَأخذ مشقصا فقطع ودجيه فَمَاتَ فَرَآهُ الطُّفَيْل فِي الْمَنَام فَقَالَ مَا فعل الله بك قَالَ غفر لي بهجرتي ال النَّبِي صلى الله عَلَيْهِ وَسلم قَالَ مَا شَأْن يَديك قَالَ قيل انا لَا نصْلح مِنْك مَا أفسدت يَديك فقصها الطُّفَيْل على النَّبِي صلى الله عَلَيْهِ وَسلم فَقَالَ اللَّهُمَّ وليديه فَاغْفِر وَرفع يَدَيْهِ

أخرجه مُسلم فِي الصَّحِيح

Al-Bukhārī said, in *al-Adab al-Mufrad,* in the Book on Raising One's Hands in Prayer:

> Ḥammād ibn Zayd narrated to us that Ḥajjāj al-Ṣawāf narrated to him from Abū Zubayr from Jābir ibn ʿAbdullāh that Ṭufayl ibn ʿAmr said to the Prophet, 'Do you need a fortress? The fortress of Dūs is impenetrable.' But the Messenger of Allah ﷺ refused because Allah had provided him with the Anṣār. So,

25

Ṭufayl migrated along with another man from his people. That man fell ill. He became impatient and took a sharp arrow, cutting with it his knuckles and he passed away. Ṭufayl saw him in a dream and said, 'How did Allah treat you?' He said, 'He forgave me for my migration to the Prophet ﷺ.' He said, 'What is wrong with your hands?' He said, 'It was said to me, "I will not remove from you that which you did to your hands."' Ṭufayl informed the Prophet ﷺ of that and he said, 'O, Allah! forgive even his hands' and he raised his hands.

Muslim narrated it in his *al-Ṣaḥīḥ*.

# 26

## حَدِيث ثَان عَنهُ

## A SECOND HADITH OF JĀBIR

قَالَ الامام أَحْمد

٢٦ - حَدثنَا حُسَيْن حَدثنَا ابْن أبي ذِئْب عَن رجل من بني سَلمَة عَن جَابر بن عبد الله أَن النَّبِي أَتَى مَسْجِد الْأَحْزَاب فَوضع رِدَاءَهُ وَقَامَ وَرفع يَدَيْهِ يَدْعُو عَلَيْهِم وَلم يصل ثمَّ جَاءَ ودعا عَلَيْهِم وَصلى

Imam Aḥmad said:

Ḥusayn narrated to us that Ibn Abī Dhi'b narrated to him from a man from Banī Salamah, from Jābir ibn ʿAbdullāh that the Prophet ﷺ came to the mosque of the confederates and took off his outer garment. He got up and raised his hands, supplicating against them, and did not pray. Then he came and supplicated against them and prayed.

# 27

## حَدِيث ثَالِث عَنهُ

## A THIRD HADITH OF JĀBIR:

قَالَ الطَّبَرَانِيّ فِي الْأَوْسَط

٢٧ - حَدثنَا عبد الله بن أَحْمد حَدثنَا عبيد الله بن معَاذ حَدثنَا أبي حَدثنَا سُفْيَان عَن يُوسُف بن مُحَمَّد بن الْمُنْكَدر عَن أَبِيه عَن جَابر رَضِي الله عَنهُ قَالَ قَالَ رَسُول الله صلى الله عَلَيْهِ وَسلم ان الله عز وَجل حَيّ كَرِيم يستحي من عَبده أَن يرفع اليه يَدَيْهِ فيَردهُمَا صفرا لَيْسَ فيهمَا شَيْء. رِجَاله رجال الصَّحِيح الا يُوسُف وَهُوَ ثِقَة

Al-Ṭabarānī said in his *Awsaṭ:*

> ʿAbdullāh ibn Aḥmad narrated to us that ʿUbayd ibn Muʿādh narrated to him that his father narrated to him that Sufyān narrated on the authority of Yūsuf ibn Muḥammad ibn al-Munkadar on the authority of his father that Jābir *(raḍiyallāhu ʿanhu) said*, 'The Messenger of Allah ﷺ said, "Allah (*ʿazza wa jall)* is very Bashful and Generous. He is too bashful before His slave than that the latter should raise his hands towards Him, and He should return them to him empty without giving him something."'

Its narrators are men of the *ṣaḥīḥ*, except Yūsuf, but he is trustworthy.

## 28

# حديث حُصَيْن بن وحوح الأَنْصارِيّ رضى الله عَنهُ

# A HADITH OF ḤUSAYN IBN WAḤŪḤ AL-ANṢĀRĪ *(RAḌIYALLĀHU ʿANHU)*

قَالَ الطَّبَرَانِيّ

٢٨ - حَدثنَا مُوسَى بن هَارُون حَدثنَا عمر بن زُرَارَة حَدثنَا عِيسَى بن يُونُس عَن سعيد بن عُثْمَان البلوي عَن عُرْوَة بن سعيد الأَنْصارِيّ عَن أَبِيه عَن حُصَيْن بن وحوح أَن طَلْحَة بن الْبَراء توفّي فَدفن بِاللَّيْلِ فَأخْبر النَّبِي صلى الله عَلَيْهِ وَسلم حِين أصبح فجَاء حَتَّى وقف على قَبره فصف النَّاس مَعَه ثمَّ رفع يَدَيْهِ فَقَالَ اللَّهُمَّ الق طَلْحَة تضحك اليه ويضحك اليك

Al-Ṭabarānī said:

> Mūsā ibn Hārūn narrated to us that ʿUmar ibn Zurārah narrated to him that ʿĪsā ibn Yūnus narrated to him on the authority of Saʿīd ibn ʿUthmān al-Balawī from ʿUrwah ibn Saʿīd al-Anṣārī from his father, on the authority of Ḥusayn ibn Waḥūḥ that Ṭalḥah ibn al-Barāʾ passed away and was buried at night. The Prophet ﷺ was informed when he awakened. So, he went until he stood over his grave and people lined up with him. Then, he raised his hands saying, 'O, Allah! Meet Ṭalḥah, smiling at him and he at You.'

29

# حَدِيث خَالِد بن عرطفة رَضِي الله عَنهُ

## A HADITH OF KHĀLID IBN ʿURṬAFAH (*RAḌIYALLĀHU ʿANHU)*

قَالَ الطَّبَرَانِيّ

٢٩ - حَدثنَا أَبُو خَالِد الْبَزَّاز عَن خَالِد بن عرطفة قَالَ رَأَيْت رَسُول الله صلى الله عَلَيْهِ وَسلم رَافعا يَدَيْهِ يَقُول اللَّهُمَّ بَارك على خيل أحمس ورجالها

Al-Ṭabarānī said, ʻAbū Khālid al-Bazzār narrated that Khālid ibn ʿUrṭafah said, "I saw the Messenger of Allah ﷺ raising his hands saying, ʻO, Allah! Bless the horses and the men of Aḥmas.'"'

30

# حَدِيث عبد الله بن عَبَّاس رَضِي الله عَنهُمَا

# A HADITH OF ʿABDULLĀH IBN ʿABBĀS (*RAḌIYALLĀHU ʿANHUMĀ*)

قَالَ أَبُو دَاوُد

٣٠ - حَدثنَا مُوسَى بن اسماعيل حَدثنَا وهيب بن خَالِد حَدثنَا الْعَبَّاس بن عبد الله بن معبد بن الْعَبَّاس بن عبد الْمطلب عَن عِكْرِمَة عَن ابْن عَبَّاس قَالَ الْمَسْأَلَة أَن ترفع يَديك حَذْو منكبيك أَو نَحْوهَا وَالِاسْتِغْفَار أَن تُشِير باصبع وَاحِد والابتهال أَن تمد يَديك جَمِيعًا تَابعه سُفْيَان عَن الْعَبَّاس وَرِجَاله رجال الصَّحِيح الاالعباس وَلَا بَأْس بِهِ

وَقَالَ حَدثنَا مُحَمَّد بن يحي بن فَارس حَدثنَا ابراهيم بن حَمْزَة حَدثنَا عبد الْعَزِيز بن مُحَمَّد عَن الْعَبَّاس بن عبد الله بن معبد بن عَبَّاس عَن أَخِيه ابراهيم بن عبد الله عَن ابْن عَبَّاس رَضِي الله عَنْهُمَا أَن رَسُول الله صلى الله عَلَيْهِ وَسلم قَالَ فَذكر نَحوه

رِجَاله أَيْضا رجال الصَّحِيح الا الْعَبَّاس

Abū Dāwūd said:

> Mūsā ibn Ismāʿīl narrated to us that Wahīb ibn Khālid narrated to him that al-ʿAbbās ibn ʿAbdullāh ibn Muʿabbad ibn al-ʿAbbās ibn ʿAbd al-Muṭṭalib

> narrated from ʿIkrimah that Ibn ʿAbbās said ʿOne asks by raising their hands until they face your shoulders or are on the same level with your shoulders. Seeking forgiveness is done by pointing with one finger and humble entreaty is that you should spread your hands altogether.'

Sufyān corroborated this tradition through al-ʿAbbās. Its narrators are the narrators of authentic traditions, except al-ʿAbbās, but there is no problem with his narrations.

He [al-Ṭabarānī] also said:

> Muḥammad ibn Yaḥyā ibn Fāris narrated to us that Ibrāhīm ibn Ḥamza narrated to him that ʿAbd al-ʿAzīz ibn Muḥammad narrate from al-ʿAbbās ibn ʿAbdullāh ibn Maʿbad ibn ʿAbbās from his brother Ibrāhīm ibn ʿAbdullāh on the authority of Ibn ʿAbbās *(raḍiyallāhu ʿanhumā)* that the Messenger of Allah ﷺ said the same.

Its narrators are narrators of authentic traditions, except al-ʿAbbās.

## حَدِيث ثَان عَنهُ

## A SECOND HADITH OF ʿABDULLĀH IBN ʿABBĀS

31

قَالَ ابْن مَاجه

٣١ - حَدثنَا أَبُو كريب وَمُحَمّد بن الصَّباح قَالَا حَدثنَا عَائِذ بن حبيب عَن صَالح بن حسان الْأَنْصَارِيّ عَن مُحَمَّد بن كَعْب الْقرظِيّ عَن ابْن عَبَّاس رَضِي الله عَنْهُمَا قَالَ قَالَ رَسُول الله صلى الله عَلَيْهِ وَسلم اذا دَعَوْت فَادع بباطن كفيك وَلَا تدع بظاهرهما فاذا فرغت فامسح بهما وَجهك

أخرجه ابْن دَاوُد وَقَالَ رُوِيَ من غير وَجه عَن مُحَمَّد بن كَعْب كلهَا ضَعِيفَة وَقَالَ شيخ الاسلام أَبُو الْفضل بن حجر فِي أَمَالِيهِ هَذَا حَدِيث حسن واشتهر فِي رِوَايَة أبي الْمِقْدَام هِشَام بن زِيَاد عَن مُحَمَّد بن كَعْب لَكِن فِي مُقدّمَة مُسلم أَنه كَانَ يحدث بِهِ أَولا عَن يحيى بن هِلَال شيخ مَجْهُول عَن مُحَمَّد بن كَعْب ثمَّ حذفه يحيى وَصَارَ يرويهِ عَن مُحَمَّد بن كَعْب وَأخرجه الْحَاكِم فِي الْمُسْتَدْرك من رِوَايَة مصادف بن زِيَاد عَن مُحَمَّد بن كَعْب قَالَ شيخ الاسلام ومصادف لَا يعرف وَأَظنهُ أَخا أبي الْمِقْدَام

Ibn Mājah said:

> Abū Kurayb and Muḥammad ibn al-Ṣabbāḥ narrated to us saying that Āʿidh ibn Ḥabīb narrated to them from Ṣāliḥ ibn Ḥassan al-Anṣārī, from Muḥammad ibn Kaʿb al-Qurẓī that Ibn ʿAbbās said, 'The Messenger

31

of Allah ﷺ said, "When you supplicate, supplicate with the palms of your hands. Do not supplicate with the backs of your hands. And when you have finished, wipe your face with them.'"

Abū Dāwūd also narrated it and said, 'It has been narrated through several chains from Muḥammad ibn Kaʿb. All of those chains are weak.' However, Sheikh al-Islām Abū al-Faḍl ibn Ḥajar said in his *Amālīh,* 'This hadith is acceptable *(ḥasan).*'

This hadith has become widespread through the narration of Abū al-Miqdām Hishām ibn Ziyād, from Muḥammad ibn Kaʿb. However, Muslim said in his *Muqaddimah* that he had first narrated it from Yaḥyā ibn Hilāl, an unknown sheikh, from Muḥammad ibn Kaʿb. Then, he removed Yaḥyā from the narration and began to narrate it from Muḥammad ibn Kaʿb directly. It was also narrated by al-Ḥākim in his *Mustadrak*, by way of Miṣādaf ibn Ziyād from Muḥammad ibn Kaʿb. Sheikh al-Islām said 'Miṣādaf is unknown. I assume he is the brother of Abū al-Miqdām.'

32

# حَدِيث ثَالِث عَنهُ

## A THIRD HADITH FROM ʿABDULLĀH IBN ʿABBĀS

٣٢ - حَدثنَا ابراهيم حَدثنَا هَارُون بن مَعْرُوف أخبرنَا عبد الْمجِيد بن عبد الحميد بن جريج الْأَسْلَمِيّ عَن حُسَيْن بن عبد الله عَن عِكْرِمَة عَن ابْن عَبَّاس رَضِي الله عَنْهُمَا قَالَ رَأَيْت رَسُول الله صلى الله عَلَيْهِ وَسلم يَدْعُو بِعَرَفَة ويداه الى صَدره كاستطعام الْمِسْكِين

Ibrāhīm narrated to us that Hārūn ibn Maʿrūf narrated to him that ʿAbd al-Majīd ibn ʿAbd al-Ḥamīd ibn Jurayj al-Aslamī informed him on the authority of Ḥusayn ibn ʿAbdullāh from ʿIkrima that Ibn ʿAbbās *(raḍiyallāhu ʿanhumā)* said, 'I saw the Messenger of Allah ﷺ supplicating at ʿArafah with his hands at chest level similar to how the indigent beg for food.'

# 33

## حَدِيث رَابع عَنهُ وَعَن أَخِيه الْفضل

## A FOURTH HADITH FROM IBN ʿABBĀS

قَالَ الامام أَحْمد فِي مُسْند عبد الله بن الْعَبَّاس

٣٣ - حَدثنَا يحيى بن سعيد عَن عبد الْملك عَن عَطاء عَن ابْن عَبَّاس رَضِي الله عَنْهُمَا قَالَ أَفَاضَ رَسُول الله صلى الله عَلَيْهِ وَسلم من عَرَفَة وردفه أُسَامَة بن زيد فجالت النَّاقة وَهُوَ رَافع يَدَيْهِ لَا يجاوزان رَأسه

Imam Aḥmad said in his *Musnad,* in the section of the narrations from ʿAbdullāh ibn al-ʿAbbās:

> Yaḥyā ibn Saʿīd narrated to us from ʿAbd al-Malik, from ʿAtā' that Ibn ʿAbbās *(raḍiyallāhu ʿanhu)* said, 'The Messenger of Allah ﷺ departed ʿArafah and Usāmah ibn Zayd came up behind him. His she-camel began to walk while he was raising his hands and not turning his head about.'

34

# حَدِيث الْفضل بن عَبَّاس رَضِي الله عَنْهُمَا

# A HADITH OF AL-FAḌL IBN ʿABBĀS (*RAḌIYALLĀHU ʿANHUMĀ*)

قَالَ الامام أَحْمد

٣٤ - حَدثنَا يعلى محم بن عبد قَالَا حَدثنَا عبد الْملك عَن عَطاء عَن عبد الله بن الْعَبَّاس عَن الْفضل قَالَ أَفَاضَ رَسُول الله صلى الله عَلَيْهِ وَسلم من عَرَفَات وَأُسَامَة بن يزِيد ردفه فَجَالَتْ النَّاقة وَهُوَ وَاقِف بِعَرَفَات قبل أَن يفِيض وَهُوَ رَافع يَدَيْهِ لَا يجاوزان رَأسه

Imam Aḥmad said:

> Yaʿlā and Muḥammad, both sons of ʿUbayd narrated to us, saying that ʿAbd al-Malik narrated to them from ʿAtā' from ʿAbdullāh ibn ʿAbbās that al-Faḍl said, 'The Messenger of Allah ﷺ departed from ʿArafat. Usāmah ibn Zayd came up from behind him. His she-camel began to walk while he was standing at ʿArafat before he departed. He was raising his hand and not moving his head about.'

## حَدِيث ثَان عَنهُ

## A SECOND HADITH FROM AL-FAḌL

قَالَ الامام أَحْمد

٣٥ - حَدثنَا عَليّ بن اسحاق أخبرنَا عبد الله بن مبارك أخبرنَا لَيْث بنن سعد حَدثنَا عبد ربه بن سعيد عَن عمرَان بن أبي أنس عَن عبد الله بن نَافِع بن العمياء عَن ربيعَة بن الْحَارِث عَن الْفضل بن عَبَّاس رَضِي الله عَنْهُمَا قَالَ قَالَ رَسُول الله صلى الله عَلَيْهِ وَسلم الصَّلَاة مثنى مثنى تشهد فِي كل رَكْعَتَيْنِ وتضرع وتخشع وتمسكن ثمَّ تقنع يديك يَقُول ترفعهما الى رَبك مُسْتَقْبلا ببطونهما وَجهك وَتقول يَا رب يَا رب فَمن لم يفعل ذَلِك فَقَالَ فِيهِ قولا شَدِيدا

ʿAlī ibn Isḥāq narrated to us that ʿAbdullāh ibn Mubarak informed him that Layth ibn Saʿd informed him that ʿAbd Rabbahu ibn Saʿīd narrated to him from ʿImran ibn Abī Anas from ʿAbdullāh ibn Nāfi' ibn al-ʿUmyā' from Rabīʿah ibn al-Ḥārith that al-Faḍl ibn ʿAbbās (*raḍiyallāhu ʿanhumā)* said:

> The Messenger of Allah ﷺ said, 'Prayer is two by two. There is a tashahhud after every two rakʿahs. One should show humility, lowliness and submissiveness. Then, he should hide himself in his hands, meaning that he should raise them to his Lord, facing his palms, saying, "My Lord! My Lord!" If anyone does not do that, he is ____.' And he mentioned some harsh words.

# 36

## حَدِيث يزِيد سعيد الْكِنْدِيّ رَضِي الله عَنهُ

## A HADITH OF YAZĪD IBN SA'ĪD AL-KINDĪ *(RAḌIYALLĀHU 'ANHU)*

قَالَ أَبُو دَاوُد

٣٦ - حَدثنَا ابْن قُتَيْبَة بن سعيد حَدثنَا ابْن لَهِيعَة عَن حَفْص بن هِشَام بن عتبَة بن أبي وقاس عَن السَّائِب بن يزِيد عَن أَبِيه أَن النَّبِي صلى الله عَلَيْهِ وَسلم كَانَ اذا دَعَا فَرفع يَدَيْهِ مسح وَجهه بيدَيْهِ

Abū Dāwūd said:

> Qutaybah ibn Sa'īd narrated that Ibn Luhay'ah narrated to him from Ḥafṣ ibn Hāshim ibn 'Utbah ibn Abī Waqqāṣ, from al-Sā'ib ibn Yazīd from his father that the Prophet ﷺ would, when he supplicated, raise his hands and wipe his face with them.

# 37

# حَدِيث الْبَرَاء بن عَازِب رَضِي الله عَنهُ

## ABŪ YAʿLĀ SAID IN HIS *MUSNAD AL-KABĪR:*

قَالَ أَبُو يعلى فِي مُسْنده الْكَبِير

٣٧ - حَدثنَا عبد الْوَاحِد بن غياث حَدثنَا عبد الحميد بن زُرَيْق حَدثنَا ابْن دَاوُد الْأَعْمَى عَن الْبَرَاء بن عَازِب عَن النَّبِي صلى الله عَلَيْهِ وَسلم أَنه كَانَ اذا أَصَابَته شدَّة دَعَا وَرفع يَدَيْهِ حَتَّى يرى بَيَاض ابطيه

ʿAbd al-Wāḥid ibn Ghiyāth narrated to us that ʿAbd al-Hamīd ibn Zurayq narrated to him that Ibn Dāwūd narrated to him that al-Aʿmā narrated to him from al-Barāʾ ibn ʿĀzib that whenever the Prophet ﷺ supplicated intensely, he would raise his hand until the whites of his underarms became visible.

# حَدِيث أبي بَرزَة رَضِي الله عَنهُ

# 38 A HADITH OF ABĪ BARAZAH (*RAḌIYALLĀHU ʿANHU*)

قَالَ أَبُو العلى

٣٨ - حَدثنَا الْحسن بن حَمَّاد حَدثنَا ابْن فُضَيْل عَن يزِيد بن أبي زِيَاد عَن سُلَيْمَان بن عَمْرو بن الأحوض حَدثنِي أَبُو هِلَال عَن صَاحب هَذِه الدَّار عَن أبي برزه الْأَسْلَمِيّ أَن النَّبِي كَانَ يرفع يَدَيْهِ فِي الدُّعَاء حَتَّى يرى بَيَاض ابطيه. قَالَ الهيثمي رِجَاله ثِقَات لَكِن أَبُو هِلَال لَا أعرفهُ أخرجه ابْن أبي شيبَة فِي الْمُصَنّف عَن ابْن فُضَيْل بِلَفْظٍ دَعَا على رجلَيْنِ فَرفع يَدَيْهِ

Abū Yaʿlā said:

> Al-Ḥasan ibn Ḥammād narrated to us that Ibn Fuḍayl narrated from Yazīd ibn Abī Ziyād from Sulayman ibn ʿAmr ibn al-Aḥwaḍ that Abū Hilāl narrated to him from the owner of this house, from Abū Barazah al-Aslamī that the Prophet ﷺ used to raise his hands in supplication until the whites of his underarms would become visible.

Al-Haythamī said, 'Its narrators are trustworthy however, I do not know Abū Hilāl.' It was also narrated by Ibn Abī Shaybah in his *Musannaf* on the authority of Ibn Fuḍayl with the wording, '[the Prophet ﷺ] supplicated against two men and raised his hands ...'

39

# حَدِيث خَالِد بن الْوَلِيد

## AL-ṬABARĀNĪ SAID IN HIS *KABĪR*:

قَالَ الطَّبَرَانِيّ فِي الْكَبِير

٣٩ - حَدثنَا أَحْمد بن عَمْرو الْخلال الْمَكِّيّ حَدثنَا يَعْقُوب بن حميد بن كاسب حَدثنَا عبد الله بن عبد الله الْأمَوِي حَدثنَا اليسع بن الْمُغيرَة عَن أَبِيه عَن خَالِد بن الْوَلِيد رَضِي الله عَنهُ أَنه شكا الى رَسُول الله صلى الله عَلَيْهِ وَسلم الضّيق فِي مَسْكَنه فَقَالَ ارْفَعْ يديك الى السَّمَاء واسأل الله السعَة

اسناده حسن

Al-Ṭabarānī said in *al-Kabīr*:

> Aḥmad ibn ʿAmr al-Khilāl al-Makkī narrated to us that Yaʿqūb ibn Ḥamīd ibn Kāsib narrated to him that ʿAbdullāh ibn ʿAbdullāh al-Umawī narrated to him that al-Yasaʿ ibn al-Mughirah narrated from his father, from Khālid ibn al-Walīd (raḍiyallāhu ʿanhu) that he complained to the Messenger of Allah ﷺ that his living conditions were difficult. He responded, 'Raise your hands toward the heavens and ask Allah for increase.'

Its chain of transmission is acceptable [*ḥasan*].

## حَدِيث جرير رَضِي الله عَنهُ

## A HADITH OF JARĪR *(RAḌIYALLĀHU ʿANHU)*:

# 40

قَالَ أَيْضا

٤٠ - حَدثنَا أَحْمد بن زُهَيْر بن التسترِي حَدثنَا معمر بن سهل حَدثنَا عمر بن مدرك حَدثنَا مُحَمَّد بن عبيد الله عَن الشاسي عَن عبيد الله عَن جرير قَالَ رَأَيْت رَسُول الله صلى الله عَلَيْهِ وَسلم وَاقِفًا بِعَرَفَة متأبطا رِدَاءَهُ رَافعا يَدَيْهِ لَا يجاوزان رَأسه وعضلتاه ترعدان

مُحَمَّد بن عبيد الله الْعَرْزَمِي ضَعِيف

Al-Ṭabarānī also said:

> Aḥmad ibn Zuhayr ibn al-Tustarī narrated to us that Muʿammar ibn Sahl narrated that ʿUmar ibn Mudrik narrated that Muḥammad ibn ʿUbayd Allāh narrated from al-Shāsī, from ʿUbayd Allāh that Jarīr said, 'I saw the Messenger of Allah ﷺ standing at ʿArafah, draping his overgarment over his shoulders and raising his hands. He didn't turn his head from side to side. His muscles were trembling.'

Muḥammad ibn ʿUbayd Allāh al-ʿArzamī is a weak narrator.

# 41

حَدِيث أبي سعيد الخُدْرِيّ رَضِي الله عَنهُ

## A HADITH OF ABŪ SAʿĪD AL-KHUDRĪ *(RAḌIYALLĀHU ʿANHU)*

قَالَ ابْن أبي شيبَة فِي المُصَنّف

٤١ - حَدثنَا ابْن ادريس عَن مُحَمَّد بن اسحاق عَن عَاصِم عَن عمر بن قَتَادَة عَن مَحْمُود بن لبيد عَن أبي سعيد الخُدْرِيّ قَالَ قَالَ رَسُول الله صلى الله عَلَيْهِ وَسلم لَو سلك النَّاس وَاديا وشعبا وسلكتم وَاديا وشعبا لَسَلَكْت واديكم وشعبكم أَنْتُم شعار وَالنَّاس دثار وَلَوْلَا الْهِجْرَة لَكُنْت امْرأ من الْأَنْصَار ثمَّ رفع يَدَيْهِ حَتَّى أَنِّي لأرى بَيَاض ابطيه مَا تَحت مَنْكِبَيْه فَقَالَ اللَّهُمَّ اغْفِر للْأَنْصَار ولأبناء الْأَنْصَار ولأبناء أَبنَاء الْأَنْصَار

Ibn Abī Shaybah said in his *Muṣannif*: Ibn Idrīs narrated to us from Muḥammad ibn Isḥāq, from ʿĀṣim from ʿUmar ibn Qatādah from Maḥmūd ibn Labīd that Abū Saʿīd al-Khudrī said:

> The Messenger of Allah ﷺ said, 'If mankind were to travel to one valley or mountain pass and you were to travel to another, I would travel to the mountain pass and valley where you were. You are the crème while everyone else is ordinary.' He then raised his hands until I saw the whites of his underarms and said, 'O, Allah! Forgive the Anṣār, the children of the Anṣār and the Anṣār's children's children.'

# حَدِيث عبد الله بن الزبير رَضِي الله عَنهُ

# 42 A HADITH OF ʿABDULLĀH IBN AL-ZUBAYR *(RAḌIYALLĀHU ʿANHU)*

قَالَ ايضا

٤٢ - عَن مُحَمَّد بن يحيي الْأَسْلَمِيّ قَالَ رَأَيْت عبد الله بن الزبير وَرَأى رجلا رَافعا يَدَيْهِ يَدْعُو قبل أَن يفرغ من صلَاته فَلَمَّا فرغ مِنْهَا قَالَ ان رَسُول الله صلى الله عَلَيْهِ وَسلم لم يكن يرفع يَدَيْهِ حَتَّى يفرغ من صلَاته

رجال ثِقَات

Ibn Abī Shaybah also said:

> Muḥammad ibn Yaḥyā al-Aslamī said, 'I saw ʿAbdullāh ibn al-Zubayr while he was looking at a man who was raising his hands in supplication before he finished his prayer. When he finished, he said to him, "The Messenger of Allah ﷺ would not raise his hands until he finished his prayer."'

Its narrators are trustworthy.

# 43

حَدِيث أبي بكرَة رَضِي الله عَنهُ

A HADITH OF ABŪ BAKRAH (*RAḌIYALLĀHU ʿANHU)*

قَالَ أَيْضا

٤٣ - حَدثنَا زَكَرِيَّا السَّاجِي أخبرنَا عمار بن خَالِد الوَاسِطِيّ حَدثنَا الْقَاسِم بن مَالك الْمُزنِيّ عَن خَالِد الْحذاء عَن أبي بكرَة أَن رَسُول الله صلى الله عَلَيْهِ وَسلم قَالَ سلوا الله ببطون أكفكم وَلَا تسألوه بظهورها

رِجَاله رجال الصَّحِيح الا عمار وَهُوَ ثِقَة

He also said:

> Zakariyyā al-Sājī narrated that ʿAmmār ibn Khālid al-Wāsiṭī informed him that al-Qāsim ibn Mālik al-Muzanī narrated form Khālid al-Ḥadhā' that Abū Bakrah narrated that the Messenger of Allah ﷺ said, 'Ask Allah with the palms of your hands. And don't ask him with the backs of your hands.'

Its narrators are narrators of authentic [*ṣaḥīḥ*] traditions, except ʿAmmār. Nevertheless, he is trustworthy.

# حَدِيث السَّائِب بن خَلاد بن سُوَيْد بن ثَعْلَبَة الأَنْصَارِيّ

## 44 A HADITH OF AL-SA'IB IBN KHALĀD IBN SUWAYD IBN THAʿLABAH AL-ANṢĀRĪ

قَالَ أَيْضا

٤٤ - عَن خَلاد بن السَّائِب عَن أَبِيه أَن سَوَّل الله كَانَ اذا دَعَا رفع راحتيه الى وَجهه

حَفْص مَجْهُول

He also said:

> Khalād ibn al-Sa'ib narrated from his father that the Messenger of Allah ﷺ used to raise his palms to his face whenever he supplicated.

Hafṣ is an unknown narrator.

# 45 حَدِيث سعد بن أَبِي وَقاص رَضِي اللهُ عَنهُ

# A HADITH OF SAʿD IBN ABĪ WAQQĀṢ *(RAḌIYALLĀHU ʿANHU)*

قَالَ أَبُو دَاوُد

٤٥ - حَدثنَا أَحْمد بن صَالح حَدثنَا ابْن أبي فديك حَدثنَا مُوسَى ابْن يَعْقُوب عَن ابْن عُثْمَان وَهُوَ يحيي بن الْحسن بن عُثْمَان عَن أَشْعَث بن اسحاق بن سعد عَن عَمه عَامر بن سعد عَن أَبِيه سعد بن أبي وقاس قَالَ خرجنَا مَعَ رَسُول الله صلى الله عَلَيْهِ وَسلم من مَكَّة يُرِيد الْمَدِينَة فَلَمَّا كُنَّا قَرِيبا من عزورا نزل ثمَّ رفع يَدَيْهِ ثمَّ دَعَا الله سَاعَة

Abū Dāwūd said:

> Aḥmad ibn Ṣaliḥ narrated to us that Ibn Abī Fadayk narrated to him that Mūsā ibn Yaʿqūb narrated to him from Ibn ʿUthmān, who is Yaḥyā ibn al-Ḥasan ibn ʿUthmān from Ashʿath ibn Isḥāq ibn Saʿd from his paternal uncle ʿĀmir ibn Saʿd, that his father Saʿd ibn Abī Waqqāṣ said, 'We departed from Makkah with the Messenger of Allah ﷺ, on the way to Madinah. When we came near to ʿAzwarā, he descended his mount, raised his hands, and supplicated to Allah for an hour.'

# 46

## حَدِيث يزِيد بن عَامر رَضِي الله عَنهُ

## A HADITH OF YAZĪD IBN ʿĀMIR *(RAḌIYALLĀHU ʿANHU)*

قَالَ فِي الْأَوْسَط

٤٦ - حَدثنَا مِقْدَام حَدثنَا خَالِد بن نزار حَدثنَا سعيد بن السَّائِب عَن أبي الْخلف عبيد بن سعد السوَائِي عَن يزِيد بن عَامر رَضِي الله عَنهُ أَن رَسُول الله صلى الله عَلَيْهِ وَسلم أقبل وَمَعَهُ نفر حَتَّى وقف على الْقرب دون المريطى رَافعا يَدَيْهِ مُسْتَقْبلا الْقبْلَة يدْعُو

قَالَ الهيثمي رِجَاله ثِقَات الا أَن عبيدا لم أعرفهُ

Al-Ṭabarānī said in his *Awsaṭ:*

> Miqdām narrated to us that Khālid ibn Nazzār narrated to him that Saʿīd ibn al-Saʾib narrated from Abū al-Khalaf ʿUbayd ibn Saʿd al-Sawāʾī from Yazīd ibn ʿĀmir *(raḍiyallāhu ʿanhu),* that the messenger of Allah ﷺ set out with a caravan until he reached [the mountain] al-Qarn. He stopped under a barren tree, raising his hands, facing the *qiblah* and supplicating.

Al-Haythamī said, ʻIts narrators are all trustworthy, except ʻUbayd. I do not know him.ʼ

47

# حَدِيث أم عَطِيَّة رَضِي الله عَنْهَا

# A HADITH OF UMM ʿATIYYAH *(RAḌIYALLĀHU ʿANHĀ)*

٤٧ - قَالَ التِّرْمِذِيّ

حَدثنَا مُحَمَّد بن بشار وَيَعْقُوب بن ابراهيم وَغير وَاحِد كلهم عَن أبي عَاصِم عَن أبي الْجراح قَالَ حَدثنِي جَابر بن صبيح قَالَ حَدَّثتنِي أم شُرَحْبِيل قَالَت حَدَّثتنِي أم عَطِيَّة قَالَت بعث النَّبِي صلى الله عَلَيْهِ وَسلم جَيْشًا فيهم عَليّ بن أبي طَالب رَضِي الله عَنهُ فَسمِعت رَسُول الله صلى الله عَلَيْهِ وَسلم وَهُوَ رَافع يَدَيْهِ قَول اللَّهُمَّ لَا تمتني حَتَّى تريني عليا. وَقَالَ حسن غَرِيب

Al-Tirmidhī said:

> Muḥammad ibn Bashshār, Yaʿqūb ibn Ibrāhīm and others narrated to us from Abū ʿĀṣim from Abū al-Jarrāḥ who said that Jābir ibn Ṣabīḥ narrated to him that Umm Shuraḥbīl narrated to him that Umm ʿAtiyyah said, 'The Prophet ﷺ sent an army among whom was ʿAlī ibn Abī Ṭālib *(raḍiyallāhu ʿanhu)*. I heard the Messenger of Allah ﷺ saying, while raising his hands, "O, Allah! Do not take my life until You have allowed me to see Ali again."'

He (al-Tirmidhī) said, 'This is an acceptable hadith, though it is a singular narration.'

# مُرسل عبد الرَّحمَن بن محيريز

# 48 A *MURSAL*[1] NARRATION OF 'ABD AL-RAHMAN IBN MUḤAYRIZ

قَالَ مُسَدّد فِي مُسْنده

٤٨ - حَدثنَا بشر ابْن أبي الْمفضل حَدثنَا خَالِد هُوَ الْحذاء عَن أبي قلَابَة عَن عبد الرَّحْمَن بن محيريز قَالَ قَالَ رَسُول الله صلى الله عَلَيْهِ وَسلم اذا سَأَلْتُم الله فَاسْأَلُوهُ ببطون أكفكم وَلَا تسألوه بظهورها

أخرجه ابْن أبي شيبَة فِي الْمُصَنّف

Musaddad said in his *Musnad:*

> Bishr ibn Abī al-Mufaḍḍal narrated to us that Khālid al-Ḥadhā' narrated to him from Abī Qalābah that 'Abd al-Raḥmān ibn Muḥayriz said, 'The Messenger of Allah ﷺ said, "When you ask something of Allah, ask him with the palms of your hands. Don't ask him with the backs of your hands."'

Ibn Abī Shaybah narrated it in his *Muṣannaf.*

1 A mursal narration is one in which the Follower [Tābi'ī] narrates directly from the Prophet ﷺ without mentioning the Companion who narrated it to him.

# 49

# مُرسل خَلاد بن السَّائِب

# A MURSAL NARRATION OF KHALĀD IBN AL-SĀ'IB

قَالَ الامام أَحْمد

٤٩ - حَدثنَا خَلاد بن السَّائِب الْأَنْصَارِيّ أَن النَّبِي صلى الله عَلَيْهِ وَسلم كَانَ اذا سَأَلَ جعل بَاطِن كفيه اليه واذا استعاذ جعل ظُهُورهَا اليه

Imam Aḥmad said:

> Khalād ibn al-Sā'ib al-Anṣārī narrated to us that whenever the Prophet ﷺ would request something [of Allah], he would spread his palms in front of him. Whenever he would seek refuge [in Allah], he would spread the backs of his hands in front of him.

50

# مُرسل الْوَلِيد

## A *MURSAL* NARRATION OF AL-WALĪD

قَالَ الطَّبَرَانِيّ فِي الدُّعَاء

٥٠ - حَدثنَا أبي مُسلم الْكَجّي قَالَ حَدثنَا القَعْنبِي حَدثنَا عِيسَى بن يُونُس حَدثنَا ابراهيم بن يزِيد حَدثنَا الْوَلِيد بن عبد الله بن أبي مغيث قَالَ قَالَ قَالَ رَسُول الله صلى الله عَلَيْهِ وَسلم اذا دَعَا أحدكُم فَرفع يَدَيْهِ فان الله تَعَالَى جَاعل فِي يَدَيْهِ بركَة وَرَحْمَة فَلَا يردهما حَتَّى يمسح بهما وَجهه

قَالَ شيخ الاسلام فِي أَمَالِيهِ الْوَلِيد فِي طبقَة من سمع من الصَّحَابَة رَضِي الله عَنْهُم لَكِن لم أر لَهُ رِوَايَة عَن صَحَابِيّ فَيكون هَذَا الاسناد معضلا وابراهيم الرَّاوِي عَنهُ هُوَ الخوزي فِيهِ مقَال

Al-Ṭabarānī said in *al-Du ͑ā͗*:

> Abū Muslim al-Kajjī narrated to us that al-Qa ͑nabī narrated to him that ͑ Īsā ibn Yūnus narrated to him that Ibrāhīm ibn Yazīd narrated to him that al-Walīd ibn ͑Abdullāh ibn Abī Mughīth said, 'The Messenger of Allah ﷺ said, "When one of you supplicates and raises his hands, Allah (*ta ͑ālā)* begins to place mercy and blessings in his hands. He will continue to do so until he wipes his face with them both."'

Sheikh al-Islām said, in his *Amāli,* 'Al-Walīd is among those

50

who heard hadiths from the Companions *(raḍiyallāhu ʿanhum)*. However, I have not seen any hadith that he narrates from a Companion. So, the chain of this hadith is missing two narrators. In addition, Ibrāhīm who this is narrated from is a disputed narrator.'

51

# مُرْسل طاؤس

## THE *MURSAL* TRADITION OF ṬĀWUS

قَالَ عبد الرَّزَّاق فِي الْمُصَنّف

٥١ - عَن ابْن جريج عَن عَمْرو بن دِينَار سمع طاوسا يَقُول دَعَا النَّبِي على قوم فَرفع يَدَيْهِ

ʿAbd al-Razzāq said in his *Muṣannaf*:

> Ibn Jurayj said that ʿAmr ibn Dīnār heard Ṭāwus saying, 'The Prophet ﷺ supplicated against a people while raising his hands.'

# 52

## مُرْسل الزُّهْرِيّ

## MURSAL AL-ZUHRĪ

قَالَ عبد الرَّزَّاق

٥٢ - أحبرنا معمر عَن الزُّهْرِيّ كَانَ رَسُول الله يرفع يَدَيْهِ عِنْد صَدره فِي الدُّعَاء ثمَّ يمسح بهما وَجهه

ʿAbd al-Razzāq said:

> Muʿammar informed us on the authority of al-Zuhrī that the Messenger of Allah ﷺ used to raise his hands to his chest when he supplicated. Then he would wipe them over his face.

## 53

## وروى عبد الرَّزَّاق

## ʿABD AL-RAZZĀQ ALSO NARRATED THE FOLLOWING:

٥٣ - عَن معمر عَن هِشَام بن عُرْوَة عَن أَبِيه أَن رَسُول الله صلى الله عَلَيْهِ وَسلم مر بِقوم من الْأَعْرَاب كَانُوا قد أَسْلمُوا وَكَانَ الْأَحْزَاب خربت بِلَادهمْ فَرفع رَسُول الله صلى الله عَلَيْهِ وَسلم يَدْعُو لَهُم باسطا يَدَيْهِ قبل وَجهه

Muʿammar said that Hishām said that ʿUrwah narrated from his father that the Messenger of Allah ﷺ passed by a group of Bedouins who had become Muslim and the confederate tribes had destroyed their towns. So, the Messenger of Allah ﷺ raised his hands, spreading them in front of his face and prayed for them.

# 54

## وَقَالَ عبد الرزاق

## ʿABD AL-RAZZĀQ SAID:

٥٤ - أخبرنَا معمر عَن الزُّهْرِيّ قَالَ

كَانَ رَسُول الله صلى الله عَلَيْهِ وَسلم اذا أَرَادَ الْجَمْرَتَيْن وقف عِنْدهمَا وَرفع يَدَيْهِ وَلَا يفعل ذَلِك بالثالثة كَانَ اذا رمى انْصَرف

Muʿammar informed us on the authority of al-Zuhrī that whenever the Messenger of Allah ﷺ wanted to stone the first two *jamrahs*, he would stand between them and raise his hands. He would not do that with the third. Instead, after stoning he would depart.

# مُرسل مَكْحُول

# 55

## A *MURSAL* TRADITION OF MAKḤŪL

وَقَالَ عبد الرَّزَّاق

٥٥ - أخبرنَا أَبُو سعيد عبد القدوس سمع مَكْحُولًا يحدث أَن النَّبِي كَانَ اذا رأى الْبَيْت كبر وَرفع يَدَيْهِ ثمَّ يَقُول اللَّهُمَّ أَنْت السَّلَام ومنك السَّلَام فحينا رَبنَا بِالسَّلَامِ اللَّهُمَّ زد هَذَا الْبَيْت تَشْرِيفًا وتعظيما وتكريما ومهابة وَبرا وزد من شرفه وَكَرمه مِمَّن حجه واعتمره تَشْرِيفًا وتعظيما وتكريما

ʿAbd al-Razzāq said:

> Abū Saʿīd ʿAbd al-Quddūs informed us that he heard Makḥūl narrating that the Prophet ﷺ would do *takbīr* whenever he saw the House. He would then raise his hands and say, 'O, Allah! You are the Guardian of Peace. From You is all peace. Cause us, O, our Lord, to live in peace. O, Allah! increase this House in nobility, greatness, honour, splendour, and benefit. And increase whoever honours and respects it among those who perform the greater and minor pilgrimages in nobility, veneration, and honour.'

# 56

## وَقَالَ عبد الرَّزَّاق

## ʿABD AL-RAZZĀQ SAID:

٥٦ - أخبرنَا الثَّوْرِيّ عَن حبيب بن أبي ثَابت قَالَ لما رأى النَّبِي صلى الله عَلَيْهِ وَسلم الْبَيْت رفع يَدَيْهِ

Al-Thawri informed me that Ḥabīb ibn Abī Thābit said, 'When the Prophet ﷺ saw the House, he raised his hands.'

# الْمَوْقُوف على ابْن عمر وَابْن الزبير

# 57 THE *MAWQŪF*[2] TRADITION OF IBN ʿUMAR AND IBN AL-ZUBAYR

٥٧ - قَالَ البُخَارِيّ فِي الْأَدَب الْمُفْرد

حَدثنَا ابراهيم بن الْمُنْذر حَدثنَا عمر بن فليح أَخْبرنِي أبي عَن أبي نعيم وَهُوَ وهب قَالَ رَأَيْت ابْن عمر وَابْن الزبير يدعوان يديران بالراحتين على الْوَجْه

Al-Bukhārī said in *al-Adab al-Mufrad:*

> Ibrāhīm ibn al-Mundhir narrated to us that ʿUmar ibn Faliḥ narrated to him that his father informed him that Abū Naʿīm, who is Wahb, said, 'I saw Ibn ʿUmar and Ibn al-Zubayr supplicating wiping their hands over their faces.'



2 A mawqūf tradition is one that is attributed to a Companion without it being raised to a Prophetic hadith.

58

# وَقَالَ عبد الرَّزَّاق

## ʿABD AL-RAZZĀQ SAID:

٥٨ - أخبرنَا ابْن عُيَيْنَة عَن عَبَّاس بن عبد الله بن سعد قَالَ قَالَ ابْن عَبَّاس
الابتهال هَكَذَا وَبسط يَدَيْهِ وَظُهُورهمَا على وَجهه وَالدُّعَاء هَكَذَا وَرفع يَدَيْهِ
تَحت لحيته والاخلاص هَكَذَا يُشِير اصبعه

Ibn ʿUyaynah informed me, on the authority of ʿAbbās ibn ʿAbdullāh ibn Saʿd that Ibn ʿAbbās said, 'Humble entreaty is like this,' and he spread his hands and wiped the backs of them both over his face. [He then said] 'And supplication is like this,' and he raised his hands to below his beard. 'And sincerity is like this,' and he pointed with his finger.

# الْمَوْقُوف على الْحسن

## 59 THE *MAWQŪF* TRADITION OF AL-ḤASAN

قَالَ الْفرْيَابِيّ

٥٩ - حَدثنَا اسحق بن رَاهَوَيْه أخبرنَا الْمُعْتَمِر بن سُلَيْمَان قَالَ رَأَيْت أَبَا كَعْب صَاحب الْحَرِير يَدْعُو رَافعا يَدَيْهِ فاذا فرغ مسح بهما وَجهه فَقلت لَهُ من رَأَيْت يفعل هَذَا قَالَ الْحسن بن أبي الْحسن

اسناده حسن

Al-Faryābī said:

> Isḥāq ibn Rāhawayh narrated to us that al-Muʿtamir ibn Sulaymān informed him that he saw Abū Kaʿb, the silk dealer, supplicating while raising his hands. When he had finished, he wiped them over his face. I asked him, 'Who have you seen doing this?' He said, 'Al-Ḥasan ibn Abī al-Ḥasan.'

Its chain of transmission is acceptable [*ḥasan*].

وَقد قلت شعرًا

ارْفَعْ يَديك الى الرَّحْمَن مبتهلا ... واسأل سُؤال ذليل بالبكا ضرعا
فَالله أكْرم من يُرْجى وَأعظم أَن ... يرد باليأس من كفا لَهُ رفعا هَذَا آخر
الْجُزْء وَالْحَمْد لله رب الْعَالمين وَلَا حول وَلَا قُوَّة الا بِاللَّه الْعلي الْعَظِيم وَصلى
الله على خير خلقه سيدنَا مُحَمَّد وَآله وَصَحبه وَسلم آمين آمين آمين

I say, in poetic verse:

Raise your hands in humble entreaty to the Most Merciful,
And ask him as in a lowly way, crying and in humility.

For Allah is the Most Noble of those in whom people place their hopes and Greater, Than that He should return a palm that has been raised to him empty.

This is the last part of this book. All praise is due to Allah, Lord of the worlds. There is no might nor power except in Allah, the Exalted, the Great.

May Allah bless the best of creation, *Sayyidunā* Muhammad, his family and companions. *Āmīn. Āmīn. Āmīn.*

# The Etiquettes of Supplication and Invocation

This section is translated from *al-Ḥiṣn al-Ḥaṣīn* by Allamah Muhammad al-Jazarī with footnotes by Dr. ʿAbd al-Raʾūf ibn Muḥammad al-Kammālī. Unless otherwise indicated, all footnotes have been translated from the text.

Some of these etiquettes reach the level of being either a pillar or a pre-condition of supplication. Others reach one of the rest of the different levels of commanded and prohibited matters. They are:[3]

1) Avoiding illicit food, drink, clothes and income.[4]
2) Sincerity towards Allah (*ta ʿālā)*.[5]
3) Preceding it with pious acts which one may mention in

3 In this section, the author alludes to the meaning of the various hadiths that have come down regarding the etiquettes of supplication, without actually bringing out the hadiths. **Translator's note:** Dr. Kammālī relates the relevant hadiths in these footnotes.

4 This is indicated in the hadith in Muslim (hadith no. 1851) and Tirmidhī (hadith no. 2989), on the authority of Abū Hurayrah. It begins, 'Indeed, Allah is pure and accepts only the pure.' **Translator's note:** The most relevant part of the hadith to the author's words is where the narrator said, 'He then made mention of a person who is on a long journey, with his hair dishevelled and covered in dust, who lifts his hand toward the sky and supplicates, "My Lord! My Lord!" But his food is unlawful, his drink is unlawful, his clothes are unlawful, and his nourishment are unlawful. So, how can he hope for his supplication to be answered?'

5 Al-Shawkānī (*raḥmatullāhi ʿalayhi)* said, 'This is one of the most important of etiquettes related to the response to one's supplication, because sincerity is the axis around which acceptance revolves. He [Allah] *(ʿazza wa jall)* has said: *'And call upon Allah making your religion exclusively for His sake' (Ghāfir* 40: 14). Thus, if someone supplicates his Lord without sincerity, it is certain that it will go unanswered, unless Allah grants him His grace. And He is the Possessor of immense grace."

times of difficulty.[6]

4) Cleanliness and purity.[7]

5) Ablution.[8]

6) Facing the *qiblah*.[9]

---

6 On this, there is the hadith of Ibn ʿUmar (*raḍiyallāhu ʿanhum)* on the story of the three men who entered a cave and were trapped by a boulder. They sought a means to Allah (ta ʿālā) through their pious acts. This hadith was related by Bukhārī (hadith no. 3465), Muslim (hadith no. 2099) and Abū Dāwūd (hadith no. 3387).

7 Purity [*al-taṭahhur*] includes all kinds of purification, including tayammum and instinjāʾ. About this, there is the hadith of al-Muhājir ibn Qanfadh *(raḍiyallāhu ʿanhu)*, when the Messenger of Allah ﷺ excused himself for not returning his greeting while he was urinating. He said, 'I dislike mentioning the name of Allah except in a state of purity' This was related by Abū Dāwūd (hadith no. 17), Nasāʾī (hadith no. 37), Ibn Mājah (hadith no. 350), Ibn Ḥibbān (hadith nos. 803 and 806), and Ḥākim (hadith no. 167), who declared it authentic. And al-Dhahabī agreed.

8 There is a long hadith related on the authority of Abū Mūsā al-Ashʿarī (*raḍiyallāhu ʿanhu)*, in which he mentioned that when the Prophet ﷺ wanted to seek forgiveness for ʿUbayd Abū ʿĀmir, he performed ablution and then raised his hands. It was narrated by Bukhārī (hadith nos. 41-42) and Muslim (hadith nos. 1943-1944). There is also the hadith of ʿUthmān ibn Ḥunayf regarding the story of the blind man that asked the Messenger of Allah ﷺ to pray that Allah return to him his sight. It was narrated by Tirmidhī (hadith no. 3578), Nasāʾī (hadith nos. 658-660), and Ibn Mājah (hadith no. 1385). **Translator's note:** Dr. Kammālī is referring to the famous hadith used as a proof for *tawassul* (seeking a means through the Prophet ﷺ in supplication.)

9 There are many hadiths related on this subject. One of them is the hadith of ʿUbād ibn Tamīm on the authority of his uncle,

7) Prayer.[10]

8) Kneeling on one's knees.[11]

9) Praising Allah (*ta 'ālā) at the beginning and the end.*[12]

---

'Abdullāh ibn Zayd ibn 'Āsim al-Anṣārī, about the supplication on the day the Prophet ﷺ went out to supplicate for rain. This was narrated by Bukhārī (hadith no. 1012), Muslim (hadith no. 611), Abū Dāwūd (hadith nos. 1161-1164), Tirmidhī (hadith no. 556), Nasā'ī (hadith no. 155), Ibn Mājah (hadith no. 1267), and Aḥmad (hadith no. 39).

10 Regarding this, there is the hadith of Abu Bakr (*raḍiyallāhu 'anhu),* who narrated, 'I heard the Messenger of Allah ﷺ say, "No man commits any sin, then gets up, purifies himself and then prays and seeks forgiveness of Allah, except that Allah will forgive him."' It was narrated by Abū Dāwūd (hadith no. 1521), Tirmidhī (hadith nos. 406 and 3006), Nasā'ī (hadith no. 414-417), Ibn Mājah (hadith no. 1395), Ibn Ḥibbān (hadith no. 623) and Ibn Sunnī in *'Amal al-Yawm wa al-Laylah* (hadith no. 359). There is also the abovementioned hadith of 'Uthmān ibn Ḥunayf regarding the story of the blind man.

11 Al-Shawkānī (*raḥmatullāhi 'alayhi)* said, 'Nothing has been confirmed regarding the need to do this. But something has been narrated [in an unauthenticated tradition] that indicates it from 'Awānah.'

12 Regarding this, there is the hadith of Faḍālah ibn 'Ubayd (*raḍiyallāhu 'anhu),* attributing it to the Prophet ﷺ, 'When one of you supplicates, then let him begin with the praise of his Lord (*'azza wa jall),* then prayers upon the Prophet ﷺ.' It was narrated by Abū Dāwūd (hadith no. 1481), Tirmidhī (hadith nos. 3476 and 3477), Nasā'ī (hadith no. 44), Aḥmad (18), Ibn Ḥibbān (hadith no. 196), and Ḥākim (hadith no. 230). There are many hadiths related about the Prophet ﷺ doing this, such as the hadith of Anas (*raḍiyallāhu 'anhu)* on the intercession, which was narrated by Bukhārī (hadith nos. 417-418), Muslim (hadith nos. 180-181), and

10) Sending prayers upon the Prophet ﷺ.[13]

11) Spreading one's hands.[14]

12) Raising one's hands.[15]

13) When raising one's hands, raising them to the level of one's shoulders.[16]

---

Ibn Mājah (hadith no. 4312).

13 The previously mentioned hadith of Faḍālah is evidence for this.

14 It is as if the author (*raḥmatullāhi ʿalayhi*) is alluding to the hadith of Ibn ʿAbbās which was narrated by Abū Dāwūd (hadith no. 1486) and Ḥākim (hadith no. 536), 'When you ask Allah, ask Him with the palms of your hands…' However, this hadith is very weak. Nevertheless, there are many authentic and mass transmitted hadiths on the raising of the hands, which state explicitly that one should spread their hands and not close them when supplicating.

15 The hadiths on the raising of hands in supplication are extremely plentiful. They have reached the level of mass transmission in meaning [al-tawātur al-maʿanawi]. See Kettānī's *al-Naẓm al-Mutanāthir fī al-Ḥadīth al-Mutawātir.*

16 Regarding this, there is the hadith of Ibn ʿAbbās (*raḍiyallāhu ʿanhum),* which he attributed to the Prophet ﷺ: 'Supplication is that should raise your hands up to the level of your shoulders, or nearly there, seek forgiveness and point with your finger. Humble entreaty is that you should spread your hands completely.' It was narrated by Abū Dāwūd (hadith nos. 1489-1490). There is also the hadith '"Humble entreaty is like this," and he raised his hands and place the backs of them in front of his face.' There is also the hadith of Sahl ibn Saʿd (*raḍiyallāhu ʿanhum*), 'The Messenger of Allah ﷺ would not supplicate except that he would put his hands on level with his shoulders.' This was narrated by Aḥmad (hadith no. 337) and Ḥākim (hadith no. 536).

14) Uncovering one's hands.[17]

15) Displaying proper manners.[18]

16) Showing humility.[19]

17) Displaying submission.[20]

18) Not raising one's vision towards the sky.[21]

19) Asking Allah (*ta 'ālā)* through His Beautiful Names and

---

17 In other words, not keeping them covered. This has been mentioned by al-Khaṭṭābī (*raḥmatullāhi 'alayhi)* as one of the etiquettes, as was mentioned in Ṣalāt al-Mu'min of Ibn al-Imām. Likewise, regarding uncovering both hands, al-Shawkānī *(raḥmatullāhi 'alayhi)* has stated that it was related from Ibn Mardawīhi.

18 Perhaps what the author (*raḥmatullāhi 'alayhi)* means by 'displaying proper manners' is showing humility, lowliness and submissiveness in one's supplications. Ibn al-Imām has mentioned it among the etiquettes of supplication in *Ṣalāt al-Muslim fī al-Du'ā' wa al-Dhikr.* It is also possible that the author is alluding to the hadith of Ali *(raḍiyallāhu 'anhu)* about the opening praise of the Prophet ﷺ in the prayer. That hadith was narrated by Muslim (hadith nos. 534-535), Abū Dāwūd (hadith no. 760), Tirmidhī (hadith no. 3421), and Nasā'ī (hadith no. 130).

19 Regarding this, there is the statement of Muslim ibn Yassār (*raḥmatullāhi 'alayhi),* 'If you were in front of a king, seeking a need, it would behove you to be humble towards him.' It was narrated by Ibn Abī Shaybah in his *Muṣannif,* in *Kitāb al-Zuhd.*

20 Regarding this, there is the hadith of Ibn 'Abbās (*raḍiyallāhu 'anhum)* about the Prophet ﷺ going out for the prayer of rain. It was narrated by Tirmidhī (hadith no. 558). It was also narrated by Nasā'ī (hadith no. 156) and Ibn Mājah (hadith no. 1266).

21 On this, there is the hadith of Abū Hurayrah (*raḍiyallāhu 'anhu),* narrated by Muslim (hadith no. 321) and Nasā'ī (hadith no. 39).

Lofty Attributes.[22]

20) Avoiding rhyming and affectation.[23]

21) Not beautifying one's voice as a singer.[24]

22) Seeking a means to Allah (*ta ʿālā)* through His Prophet[25]

---

22 Perhaps he is alluding to the hadith of Ibn Masʿūd (*raḍiyallāhu ʿanhu),* on the supplication for anxiety and sadness, 'O, Allah! I am your slave, son of your male slave and son of your female slave...' In that hadith, there is the statement, 'I ask you by every Name which You possess...' It was narrated by Ibn Ḥibbān (hadith no. 972).

23 On this, there is the hadith of Ibn ʿAbbās (*raḍiyallāhu ʿanhum),* narrated by Bukhārī (hadith no. 138).

24 The author (*raḥmatullāhi ʿalayhi)* alluded to a supposed narration of the Tābiʿī without giving its source. However, I did not find anything like this from the Companions or the Tābiʿīn. Nevertheless, I found some excellent words on the subject from Ibn al-Humām al-Ḥanafī (*raḥmatullāhi ʿalayhi),* in *Fatḥ al-Qadīr,* where he said, 'I do not believe that excessive beautification of one's voice in supplication, as is done by the reciters of this time, would come from someone who understands the meaning of supplication and request. Such a thing [beautifying one's voice like song] is only a form of play. That is because, if it is compared with what happens in the world, a person who requests a need from a king, while beautifying his voice with song in such a way that he raises then lowers his voice, approaches and then retreats, as is the case of singing, would no doubt be accused of ridicule and play because what is appropriate at the time of requesting one's needs is humility, not beautification.'

25 On this, there is the hadith of ʿUthmān ibn Junayf on the story of the blind man who sought that the Messenger of Allah ﷺ ask Allah to return his sight to him. We have already mentioned it.

and pious servants.[26]

23) Lowering one's voice.[27]

24) Recognizing one's sins.[28]

25) Choosing the authentic supplications of the Prophet ﷺ, because he didn't leave any need to be asked by anyone else.[29]

---

26 On this, there is the hadith of Anas (*raḍiyallāhu ʿanhu),* narrated in Bukhārī (hadith no. 494), that whenever ʿUmar ibn al-Khaṭṭāb *(raḍiyallāhu ʿanhu)* would ask for rain, he would do so through al-ʿAbbās ibn ʿAbd al-Muṭṭalib, saying, 'O, Allah! We used to seek a means to You through Your Prophet and you granted us rains. And now we seek a means to You through the uncle of the Prophet. So, grant us rain.' He [Anas] said, 'And they would receive rain.'

27 Regarding this, there is the hadith of Abū Mūsā al-Ashʿarī (*raḍiyallāhu ʿanhu),* that was narrated by Bukhārī (hadith no. 187), Muslim (hadith no. 2076), Abū Dāwūd (hadith nos. 1526-1528), Tirmidhī (hadith no. 3374), Nasā'ī (hadith nos. 537 and 538), Ibn Mājah (hadith no. 3824), and Aḥmad (hadith nos. 394, 402 and 418).

28 There are various hadiths that relate to this, including the hadith of Abu Bakr al-Ṣiddīq (*raḍiyallāhu ʿanhu), 'Say: O, Allah! I have wronged myself with much wrong...'* This hadith was narrated by Bukhārī (hadith no. 317), Muslim (hadith no. 2078), Tirmidhī (hadith no. 3531), Nasā'ī (hadith no. 53), Ibn Mājah (hadith no. 3835), and Aḥmad (hadith nos. 4 and 7).

29 On this, there is the hadith of Abū Bakrah (*raḍiyallāhu ʿanhu),* when he supplicated, that he used to supplicate three times in the morning and three times in the evening, 'O, Allah! Grant me wellbeing in my body...' He was following the Prophet ﷺ in that. This was narrated by Abū Dāwūd (hadith no. 5090) and Nasā'ī (hadiths nos. 22 and 572). Its chain is *ḥasan.*

26) Choosing comprehensive supplications.[30]

27) Beginning by supplicating for oneself and supplicating for one's parents and believing brethren.[31]

28) Not supplicate only for himself if he is an Imam.[32]

29) Asking with earnestness.[33]

---

30 Regarding this, there is the hadith of ʿĀ'ishah (*raḍiyallāhu ʿanhā),* which was narrated by Abū Dāwūd (hadith no. 1482).

31 The author (*raḥmatullāhi ʿalayhi)* alluded to what is in Muslim, although all that he related was the supplication for another person, Ṣafwān said:

I arrived in Sham and came to the house of Abū Dardā'. He wasn't home but Umm Dardā' was. She said, 'Do you intend to perform Hajj this year?' I said, 'Yes.' She said, 'Then request good for us from Allah. For the Prophet ﷺ used to say, "The supplication of a Muslim for his brother, in the latter's absence, is accepted. [When he supplicates], there is an Angel sitting over him. Every time he requests good for his brother, the Angel says, 'Āmīn. And may you have the same.'"'

It was narrated by Muslim (hadith no. 2094). As for beginning with oneself in supplication, there is the hadith of Ubay ibn Kaʿb *(raḍiyallāhu ʿanhu),* the majority of which was narrated in Muslim (hadith no. 1847). However, the version that contains the evidence for this etiquette was narrated in Abū Dāwūd (hadith no. 3984) and Tirmidhī (hadith no. 3385) that 'the Messenger of Allah ﷺ would, when he was asked to supplicate for someone, begin with himself.'

32 Regarding this, there is the hadith of Thawbān (*raḍiyallāhu ʿanhu*), narrated by Abū Dāwūd (hadith no. 90), Tirmidhī (hadith no. 357), and Ibn Mājah (hadith no. 923).

33 On this, there is the hadith of Abū Hurayrah (*raḍiyallāhu ʿanhu*) that was narrated by Bukhārī (hadith no. 139), Muslim (hadith no. 2064), Abū Dāwūd (hadith no. 1483), Tirmidhī (hadith no. 3497), Nasā'ī (hadith nos. 582 and 583), Ibn Mājah (hadith no. 3854), and

30) Supplicating with purposeful yearning.[34]

31) Supplicating from one's heart with earnestness and striving. And that one has presence of heart and a beautiful hope.[35]

32) Repeating one's supplication at least three times[36] and insisting on what one is asking for.[37]

33) Not supplicating for anything sinful or for the cutting of ties of kinship.[38]

---

Aḥmad (hadith nos. 463, 464, 486, 500 and 530).

34 Regarding this, there is the hadith of Abū Hurayrah (*raḍiyallāhu ʿanhu*), 'When one of you supplicates, let him not say, "O, Allah! forgive me if You so will." Rather let him be firm in his request and have immense desire. For, nothing that Allah gives is difficult for him.' It was narrated by Muslim (hadith no. 2063) and Ibn Ḥibbān (hadith no. 896).

35 On this, there is the hadith of Abū Hurayrah (*raḍiyallāhu ʿanhu*), narrated by Tirmidhī (hadith no. 3479) and Ḥākim (hadith no. 493), 'Call upon Allah while you are sure of his answer. Indeed, Allah does not accept the supplication of a heart that is distracted and negligent.'

36 There are many hadiths regarding this etiquette. From them is the hadith of Ibn Masʿūd (*raḍiyallāhu ʿanhu*) when the Prophet ﷺ prayed against Quraysh when they were troubling him. He was prostrating and said, 'O, Allah! Take care of the Quraysh.' And he repeated it three times. This hadith was narrated by Bukhārī (hadith no. 349) and Muslim (hadith no. 1418). Muslim added, 'And whenever he would supplicate, he would supplicate three times. Whenever he requested anything, he requested it three times.'

37 The author (*raḥmatullāhi ʿalayhi*) seems to be alluding to the hadith of ʿAbdullāh ibn Jaʿfar (*raḍiyallāhu ʿanhum*), narrated by Ibn al-Imām in *Ṣalāt al-Mu'min*.

38 On this, there is the hadith of Abū Hurayrah (*raḍiyallāhu 'anhu*)

34) That one does not pray for a matter that has been concluded.[39]

35) That one does not transgress in their supplication by supplicating for something impossible.[40]

36) That one does not exclude anyone from good.[41]

37) That one asks for all their needs.[42]

38) That the supplicant and the one who is listening both say

---

narrated by Muslim (hadith no. 2096) and Tirmidhī (hadith no. 3677).

39 Regarding this, there is the hadith of Ibn Masʿūd (*raḍiyallāhu ʿanhu),* narrated by Muslim (hadith no. 2051), about the supplication of Umm Ḥabībah, the wife of the Prophet ﷺ, that Allah allow her to enjoy [the company of] the Messenger of Allah ﷺ, her father, Abū Sufyān, and her brother Muʿāwiyah. The Prophet ﷺ explained to her that it was more appropriate for her to supplicate seeking refuge from the punishment of the Fire and of the Grave.

40 Ibn ʿAbbās (*raḍiyallāhu ʿanhum)* said, regarding the words of Allah *(ta ʿālā) 'He does not like the transgressors' (al-Aʿrāf* 7: 55), 'Both in one's supplications and in other matters.' This was narrated by Bukhārī (7/297) without a chain of transmission. But Ibn Jarīr narrated it with its complete chain of narration in his *tafsīr*.

41 On this, there is the hadith of Abū Hurayrah (*raḍiyallāhu ʿanhu),* when the Bedouin supplicated in his prayer saying, 'O, Allah! Have mercy on me and on Muhammad. But don't have mercy on anyone else.' This hadith was narrated by Bukhārī (hadith no. 438), Abū Dāwūd (Hadith no. 380), Nasāʾī (hadith no. 14), and Ibn Mājah (hadith no. 529). It was also narrated by Tirmidhī (hadith no. 147).

42 Regarding this, there is the hadith of Anas (*raḍiyallāhu ʿanhu),* that was narrated by Tirmidhī (hadith no. 3682) and Ibn Ḥibbān (hadith nos. 866, 894 and 895).

'*Āmīn*.'[43]

39) That one wipes their face with their hands after they have concluded.[44]

40) That one does not wish to hasten it by either despairing of the response or saying, 'I supplicated. But I received no response.'[45]

43 On this, there is the hadith of Abū Hurayrah (*raḍiyallāhu 'anhu)* that the Messenger of Allah ﷺ said, '*When the Imam says 'Āmīn', say, 'Āmīn.' For, if someone's saying 'Āmīn' corresponds to the 'Āmīn' of the Angels, his past sins will be forgiven.*' It was narrated by Bukhārī (hadith no. 262 and 200), Muslim (hadiths no. 306 and 307), Abū Dāwūd (hadith nos. 934-936), and Nasā'ī (hadith nos. 143 and 145). It was also narrated by Tirmidhī (hadith no. 250).

44 About this, there is the hadith of al-Sā'ib ibn Yazīd narrated by Abū Dāwūd (no. 1492) and the hadith of Umar (*raḍiyallāhu 'anhu)* narrated by Tirmidhī (hadith no. 3386) and Ḥākim (hadith no. 536). There is also the hadith of Ibn 'Abbās *(raḍiyallāhu 'anhum)* that was narrated by Abū Dāwūd (hadith no. 1485), Ibn Mājah (hadith no. 1181) and Ḥākim (hadith no. 536). **Translator's note:** Dr. Kammālī discusses the different defects in all these hadiths. However, Ibn Ḥajar (*raḥmatullāhi 'alayhi)* has declared it *ḥasan* (acceptable). And, al-Suyūṭī also alluded to its being *ḥasan*. So, Dr. Kammālī said, 'The summary is that this hadith is treated as a *ḥasan* hadith.'

45 On this, there is the hadith of Abū Hurayrah (*raḍiyallāhu 'anhu),* which was narrated by Bukhārī (hadith no. 140), Muslim (hadith no. 2096), Abū Dāwūd (hadith no. 1484), Ibn Mājah (hadith no. 3853), and Tirmidhī (hadith no. 3387).

## The Etiquettes of Remembrance and Invocation

The scholars have said that it is more fitting that the place where one invokes Allah be clean and empty. And, it is necessary that the one who is invoking observe the perfect characteristics that we mentioned above. It is also necessary that their mouth be clean. If he or she finds some stench in their breath, they should remove it with *siwāk*. If one is invoking while sitting, they should face the *qiblah,* displaying submissiveness and humility, in a state of tranquillity, dignity, and presence of heart. One should contemplate what they are invoking and try to understand its meaning. If they don't understand anything from it, they should verify its meaning.

One should not be anxious to complete large numbers through invoking rapidly. That is why it is recommended that he or she draw out their pronunciation of *'La ilaha ill Allah.'* And, they should not consider that they have done any legislated invocation, whether it is obligatory or recommended, unless one pronounces it and hears themselves pronounce it.

The best remembrance is the Qur'an, except where something else has been legislated. And the excellence of invocation is not limited to *tasbīḥ, tahlīl* and *takbīr.*[46] Rather, anyone who acts in any way in obedience to Allah (*ta 'ālā)* is a one who

46 *Tasbīḥ* is to say *'Subhān Allāh* (Allah be glorified).' *Tahlīl* is to say *'La ilaha ill Allah* (There is no god but Allah).' *Takbīr* is to say *'Allāhu Akbar* (Allah is the Greatest).'

remembers.

The scholars have said, 'If the slave adheres to reciting the invocations that have been narrated from the Prophet ﷺ in the morning and the evening, and in different situations and at different times, such as in the night and during the day, he will be among those males and females who have remembered Allah (*ta 'ālā)* a lot.'

If someone has a litany in the night or during the day, after any prayer or at any other time, and they miss it, they should make it up and perform it when they are able to do so. One should not just leave it, to confirm their adherence to it, and so that one does not take the act of making it up lightly.

## Times When Acceptance of One's Supplication is More Likely[47]

1) Laylat al-Qadar
2) The day of ʿArafah.
3) The month of Ramadan
4) The eve of Friday.
5) Friday.
6) The second half of the night.
7) The first third of the night.[48]
8) The last third of the night.
9) The middle of the night.
10) The last hour before dawn [*waqt al-saḥar*].[49]
11) The time of the prayer of Jumuʿah is the most likely time on the day of Friday. It is between the time that the Imam sits between his two sermons and the establishment of the prayer, and from the establishment of the prayer until the *salām* to end the prayer.

47 **Translator's note:** We will not provide footnotes on the following sections except where needed, because the times, states and situations of acceptance are more or less known and agreed upon.

48 On this, there is the hadith of Abū Saʿīd al-Khudrī and Abū Hurayrah (*raḍiyallāhu ʿanhumā),* narrated by Muslim (hadith no. 523).

49 About this, there is the hadith of Abū Hurayrah about the last third of the night, narrated in Muslim (hadith no. 521) and in the four Sunans and Aḥmad.

12) When one is standing in prayer.[50]

13) After the ʿAsr prayer until sunset.

14) It has also been said that one time is the last hour of the day of Jumuʿah.[51]

15) It has also been said that one time is the beginning of the time of the Fajr prayer and before the rising of the sun.

16) The time after the rising of the sun has been suggested. Abū Dharr al-Ghifārī believed that it was after the sun had risen to the length of a forearm.

I say: I believe, by joining the authentic hadiths from the Prophet ﷺ, that the time [on the Day of Jumuʿah] is the time that the Imam is reciting al-Fatihah during the prayer until he says, '*Āmīn,*' as I have explained in other places.

Al-Nawawī *(raḥmatullāhi ʿalayhi)* said, 'The authentic and most correct position, other than which no opinion is acceptable, is that which has been narrated in *al-Ṣaḥīḥ Muslim*, from Abū Mūsā al-Ashʿarī *(raḍiyallāhu ʿanhu),* who said, 'I heard the Messenger of Allah ﷺ say, regarding the hour [of acceptance] on the day of Jumuʿah, *"It is between the time that the Imam sits until the prayer begins."*'[52]

50 On this, there is the hadith of ʿAmru ibn ʿAwf al-Muzanī (*raḍiyallāhu ʿanhu),* which was narrated by Tirmidhī (hadith no. 490) and Ibn Mājah (hadith no. 1138).

51 There is the hadith of ʿAbdullāh ibn Salām (*raḍiyallāhu ʿanhu)* to Abū Hurayrah (raḍiyallāhu ʿanhu), narrated in Mālik (hadith nos. 109-110), Abū Dāwūd (hadith no. 1046) Tirmidhī (hadith no. 491), Nasāʾī (hadith no. 114-115), and Ḥākim (hadith nos. 278-279).

52 Muslim (hadith nos. 140 and 141).

## Situations Where Acceptance is More Likely

1) When the call to prayer is being made.
2) Between the *adhān* and the *iqāmah*.
3) Between the two expressions of *'Ḥayya 'ala al-Ṣalāh'* and *'Ḥayya 'ala al-Falāḥ.'*[53]
4) When the ranks have lined up (for battle) in the way of Allah.
5) When the two parties have met in battle.
6) After the obligatory prayers.
7) In prostration.
8) After reciting the Qur'an, especially after one finishes a complete recitation, and especially for the *Qārī'*.
9) When one is drinking water of Zamzam
10) When one attends a funeral.
11) When the rooster crows.
12) When the Muslims gather.
13) In the gatherings of remembrance (dhikr).
14) When the Imam recites 'وَلَا الضَّالِّين'.
15) When one closes the eyes of the defunct.
16) At the commencement of the prayer.
17) When the rain begins to fall, as narrated by al-Shāfi'ī in *al-Umm*. He narrated without mentioning the companion, saying, 'I have memorized from more than one person

53 This was narrated by Ḥākim (hadith nos. 546-547).

that one should seek an accepted supplication at that time.'

I say: There is also the time one first sees the Ka'bah and between the two mentions of Allah's name in the one hundred and twenty fourth verse of surah al-An'ām. We have learned that it is tried and tested from more than one of the people of knowledge. And, al-Hafiz 'Abd al-Razzāq al-Ras'anī related in his *tafsīr,* from Sheikh 'Amād al-Maqdisī (*raḥmatullāhi 'alayhi)*

These are the noble places. Al-Ḥasan al-Baṣrī wrote a letter to the people of Makkah. In it, he said, 'Supplications are answered in fifteen places: During *ṭawāf*, at the *multazam*[54], below the waterspout, inside of the House, at the well of Zamzam, on Ṣafā, on Marwah, during the *sa'ī*, behind the *Maqām* [of Ibrāhīm], at 'Arafāt, in Muzdalifah, in Minā, and at the three *jamarāt*.'

I say: 'And if supplications are not answered in the presence of the Prophet ﷺ, where can they be answered?'

We also have narrated a *musalsal* hadith on the acceptance of supplications at the *multazam* by way of the people of Makkah.

54 The area between the corner of the Ka'bah and its door.

## People Whose Supplication is Accepted

1) The destitute person.
2) The oppressed, even if he is a transgressor or a disbeliever.
3) The father [for his son].
4) The just leader (Imam).
5) The righteous man.
6) The righteous son for his two parents.
7) The traveller.
8) The fasting person at the time that he breaks his fast.
9) The Muslim for his brother in the latter's absence.
10) A Muslim as long as he does not supplicate for sinfulness or the cutting of ties, and as long as he does not say, 'I supplicated and did not receive a response.'

*'Indeed Allah ('azza wa jall) has people who are set free every night. Every slave from among them has an accepted supplication.'* [55]



55 This hadith was narrated by Aḥmad (Hadith no. 254).

Printed in Great Britain
by Amazon

36268494R00064